WITNESS

WITNESS

GAY AND LESBIAN CLERGY
REPORT FROM THE FRONT

Dann Hazel

Westminster John Knox Press
Louisville, Kentucky

Scripture quotations, unless otherwise indicated, are from the New Revised Standard Version of the Bible, copyright © 1989 by the Division of Christian Education of the National Council of the Churches of Christ in the U.S.A., and used by permission.

Visit the author at www.dannhazel.com.

Book design by Sharon Adams
Cover design by Kevin Darst

First edition
Published by Westminster John Knox Press
Louisville, Kentucky

This book is printed on acid-free paper that meets the American National Standards Institute Z39.48 standard. ∞

PRINTED IN THE UNITED STATES OF AMERICA

00 01 02 03 04 05 06 07 08 09 — 10 9 8 7 6 5 4 3 2 1

ISBN 0-664-25787-9

Cataloging-in-Publication information is on file at the Library of Congress.

To Josh,
Whose Inquisitive Soul
Heightens My Own.

CONTENTS

INTRODUCTION

Nervously, I walked toward the entrance of the North Charleston Coliseum amid hundreds of conservative Christians, through a maze of tables from which vendors sold books written by the featured minister and by other authors of similar political and religious beliefs. Before entering the arena, I glanced over my shoulder toward a small group of protesters who stood along the sidewalk leading to the entrance; they were carrying signs boldly stating, "Hate Is Not a Family Value."

"Hate?" a man in front of me asked his companion. "Do you feel any hate here?"

He had a point. Although I felt no hate—at least, not yet—I sensed an intellectual rigidity, an armor of defense against points of view not easily aligned with those of most of the attendees.

Lesley—my partner's niece, who had recently earned acceptance into the Southern Baptist Theological Seminary in Louisville, Kentucky—accompanied me to Pat Robertson's Christian Coalition rally in the state most receptive to his views, both political and religious. This assertion isn't a rash generalization; it's a fact that statistics easily prove. Whenever the Christian Coalition hosts its annual national conference, South Carolina sends more delegates than does any other state in the nation.

My presence at the rally was driven by curiosity. Lesley, who was visiting for an extended weekend, leaped at the chance to see Pat Robertson in the flesh. Grateful for her companionship, I purchased her a ticket. I *wanted* her to accompany me, primarily because she was comfortable with many components of this particular brand of Christianity. She would help me fit in during the pre-show dinner, catered by the Mormon-owned Marriott International corporation—a particular irony, considering many in tonight's audience would not consider Mormons to be "true Christians."

As we made our way to our table, I was impressed by the gaudy patriotism of the red, white, and blue banners adorning the coliseum—home of the Charleston Stingrays ice hockey team—as well as the mammoth ceiling-suspended television screen from which George Bush, Rush Limbaugh, Ronald Reagan, Pat Robertson, and other conservative Republicans would speak out against America's liberal scourge. At my circular table seating ten people, I sat next to a pregnant woman who sheepishly greeted me. I returned the greeting, then concentrated perhaps too self-consciously on my meal of greasy fried chicken, corn on the cob, mashed potatoes, and a brownie for dessert. Lesley easily struck up a conversation with the mother-to-be about due dates, morning sickness, and raising children in a Christian home. Suddenly, I realized how little I knew of my partner's niece—her beliefs, the way she experienced this God of hers.

I had taken a small bite from my brownie when the president of the state chapter of the Christian Coalition began her long introduction of Pat Robertson, "a king among men, and a king among kings"—an implied comparison that disturbed me as I imagined Jesus riding a donkey through the streets of Jerusalem. When Robertson stepped onto the podium, he received a protracted standing ovation. Ten minutes into his speech, I had grown so angry I could no longer sit at the table where everyone else nodded in agreement with almost every statement Robertson made. Instead, I stood against the bleachers that had been folded away to make room for the tables, the stage, and the vending areas.

"I guess you feel a little bashed after that," Lesley said, somewhat ashamedly, as I unlocked the car door for her. I assured her that although many of his comments had angered me because of their lack of basis in truth, I was grateful that she did not share many of his religious views. (In fact, Lesley moved quickly away from the fundamentalist frame of mind the more she learned of it. A couple of years later, she withdrew from the Southern Baptist Theological Seminary because of the Southern Baptist Convention's prohibition against the ordination of women.)

But what I did not confess to her—nor to anyone—was that for the first time in my life, I had been wrested from my complacency. For over thirty years, I had lived in the safety of the closet—with the exception of coming out to several relatives and close friends—and shyly retreated whenever confronted by antigay sentiment. For most of my life, I felt quite unwilling to rock the boat.

Two years later, I had the opportunity to address a gay and lesbian teachers conference in San Francisco. What moved me most was not the audience's warm, empathetic reception as I told of my experiences as a gay teacher in South Carolina, but a subsequent panel discussion about the effects of religious views on attitudes toward homosexuality. On that panel, six ministers—four of whom were gay or lesbian—addressed the repressive stance of various church traditions toward homosexuality, and largely attributed the homophobia found in schools to lessons students and their parents learned in church. Consequently, I began to reexamine a religion I no longer understood. I *once* understood it, but lately I resented the invocation of Jesus' name as a powerful weapon against gays and lesbians. My earlier predisposition to pursue spirituality had been reduced to one question: "What's the use?"

Sitting in the auditorium at the college hosting the conference and look-ing around at the stage filled with gays, lesbians, and heterosexual allies, I felt I had finally come home.

Toward the end of the panel discussion, a minister from the audience sud-denly arose. He clutched a Bible in his right hand and began to speak adamantly about the evils of homosexuality. He stated in a trembling voice that homosexuals could not be saved unless they repented and turned from the evil ways of sodomy. He assured all homosexuals in the auditorium of their ability to change. The surprised panel members listened quietly and pa-tiently.

Slowly, one minister, a member of the panel, introduced himself to the startled dissenter and reminded him that they had not only attended college together but that they had also belonged to the same fraternity. "We partied together, Roger," he said. "Do you remember that? I loved you as a brother then, and I think you loved me. I still love you." He paused, then smiled. "And I love my partner, Carl, who is sitting right there, just a few seats down from you. I am still the same man I was back then. God loved me when you and I were college friends, even though He knew I was gay. Why would God despise something He created? In fact, God and I are closer, now that I am honest."

That gentle confrontation was the beginning for me—the beginning of a reevaluation of my own identity as a human being, as a gay man, with once-strong religious beliefs. Prior to my personal reassessment, I felt I understood all along the church's stance on sexual orientation issues. Now, a serious question baffled me: With a similar understanding of ecclesiastical condem-nation, how could gay and lesbian ministers still serve the church?

But I must go back to yet another beginning, for clarity's sake.

There is no way I could have comprehended the issues of the church and human sexuality—to the extent of my meager comprehension now—had not my own history subjected me to the truths and delusions, the longings and rebukes, the celebrations and disappointments of a life powerfully and mer-cilessly shaped by Christianity. As a young man growing up in the Lutheran Church, I felt a longing for the Lord, a propensity for visions and a tenacious dedication to reading the Bible. Simultaneously, an awareness of my homo-sexuality, no matter the fervor of my resistance, was lingering at the thresh-old of consciousness. I "knew" that I could not receive Jesus' gift of salvation *and* be gay. It was this knowledge that sealed, then tainted, my dedication to all things Christian. I wanted to fool God; I was determined to twist His arm. If my faith rivaled that of any religious ascetic, then how could God—if rea-son and logic were even small divine traits—pitch me into the fires of hell? These potent fires were made real to me by ministers who, if not adept at un-derstanding theology, were more than adequate at employing descriptive im-agery. During the spring and summer months of my childhood, I would sit on my parents' front porch and listen to nearby tent evangelists stir their transient congregations to noisy self-righteousness. In the fall and winter, the neighborhood kids and I would wage imaginary war against the Commies in the same field where the tents had been pitched.

The major turning point in my faith crisis—a crisis presented by the perceived incompatibility of my Christianity and my sexual orientation—occurred not in the historic church of my childhood but in a Southern Baptist church located just around the corner from my parents' house. A junior in high school, I was a confused teenager who responded to his frequent testosterone rushes not by playing sports, picking fights, or cruising for chicks, but by telling filthy jokes to my peers. From my Aunt Sadie, whose resources seemed inexhaustible, I accumulated a repertoire of the most sexually explicit anecdotes possible. At lunch, far from the faculty monitor who would have put a stop to my shenanigans, I repeated the stories to every teenager who would listen. Predictably, my audience increased daily. The appreciative laughter and attention of my peers encouraged me to defy the small internal censor controlling my conscience. Aunt Sadie's jokes were certainly "dirty," but I added even more sexual and scatological detail. The details, I found, increased my following exponentially. I compartmentalized my religious faith and my coarse craving for popularity through logic I cannot understand, even in hindsight. Perhaps I felt that, if my deep faith could not change God's condemning mind, I would at least have something of a good time on my way to hell.

Then, a good friend invited me to Youth Night, part of a spring revival sponsored by Hunt Street Baptist Church. I will never forget that church's name, just as I won't forget the church of my baptism and subsequent confirmation—St. Paul Lutheran Church. Their names perversely acclaim their purpose: the Hunt Street Baptist Church engaged in pursuit of a few recruits; while the church of my devout parents and my unstable childhood paid homage to the apostle whose culture-bound social views continue, after so many centuries, to erode the noble values of respect, tolerance, and charity. At any rate, I accepted Melba's invitation, drove my 1964 Ford Galaxy cautiously through the narrow streets of a mill village where many poor children played, smiled at her as I slid across the pew where her guests would be counted, and waited for the spectacle to begin.

Presumptuously, I am tempted here to place myself in that particular evangelical church in the year One A.S.—After Stonewall. But rather than associate my passage into fundamentalism with the momentous 1969 drag queen rebellion against police harassment in Greenwich Village, perhaps it is better to say my conversion occurred in 1970 and required not even a second of bravery. Melba's Jonathan Edwards–type minister chose to base his sermon on a collection of biblical passages devoted to lust—specifically, homosexual lust. Years later, I would surmise that he was more annoyed by the growing number of young men in the small town of Newberry, South Carolina, who had chosen to wear their hair long, "like hippies," than by any homosexual threat. However, true to form, his message focused on those phantom homosexuals of his imagination who, always in the pursuit of carnal gratification, would identify the most vulnerable prey as those young men with long hair—some of whom sat in the sanctuary of Hunt Street Baptist Church. Long hair constituted the first step toward an evil heart; long hair invited evil into one's soul, and that evil—at least tonight—was homosexuality. At the moment of atonement, God could be expected to grab a shock of long hair, pull the head to which it was attached to Divine Eye level, then chastise the young man ferociously on the sins of improperly fitting appendages into single-purpose orifices. Then, God would release the boy into Satan's waiting arms—Satan, the expert on carnal knowledge who opened the eyes of Adam and Eve to all the pleasures of Lapserian earth. Once, humanity knew only goodness and purity; now, life's pleasures could be enjoyed only through the contrasting knowledge of life's pains.

The messages were not lost on me. Following the minister's rants, I walked forward—no, make that *shuffled*—tears streaming down my cheeks, to accept Jesus as my Lord and Savior. I wanted desperately to whisper into the minister's ear that I was homosexual—no need to tell Jesus; he already knew—but the word stuck in my throat like a husk. Instead, I admitted I was a sinner of the worst kind, then vowed to live a godly life from that moment forward. The next day, I stopped telling dirty jokes, resisted a multitude of juvenile protests, and lost most of my "friends."

For two years, I lived as an "ex-gay." Now, I can say, with certainty, I know how a "repaired homosexual" feels. In my reparative state, I buried all powerful, misdirected feelings manifested by adolescent love. The Bible called me an abomination. Didn't it? After all, my most powerful feelings of attraction, passion, and love converged on my closest male friends. Instead of attempting to understand those feelings, I channeled every energy, every passion, every neural transmission into trying to understand God.

Upon entering college, I declared my intention to the head of the religion department to major in religion and philosophy. After commencement, I would enter the seminary and become an ordained Lutheran minister. From that professor, I soon learned the myth that Lutheran congregations are more receptive to married ministers whose wives perform "critical roles" in the church—roles this theologian did not attempt to identify. Toward fulfilling this requirement, I began dating Claire, a high school friend who lived and breathed with me my struggle against my homosexual orientation for eight unbelievable years—years she waited for me to honor my promise to overcome my "drives." Finally and sensibly, she abandoned the relationship before I damaged her life irreparably. During the Claire era, I lived superficially in two worlds. Upon graduating from college, I moved to Charleston, South

Carolina, and spent two weekends a month with Claire. On alternate weekends, I partied with my gay and lesbian friends at the clubs. Sundays were no longer reserved for church, but for nursing hangovers.

In 1974, at the end of my sophomore year, I declared English as my major with a minor in secondary education. That decision required little soulsearching when the religion department head insisted on scheduling for me a battery of psychological tests, which, I was certain, would reveal me to be the sodomite I was.

In 1976, I found myself tossed into the uncertain political seas of South Carolina's education system. In the Palmetto State's schools, the self-proclaimed mission of the educrats—at least, part of it—was, and remains, to convince young South Carolinians of the evils and depravities of the homosexual "lifestyle"; in fact, health education teachers can lose their credentials if they defy the legislation into which this policy is built. (In May 1998, the reigning Miss America, an AIDS-prevention advocate, visited several South Carolina schools, where she was cautioned not to utter words such as "gay," "homosexual," "condom," and "safe sex"—restrictions she publicly labeled "ridiculous.") So, for eighteen years I taught journalism and American and British literature to reluctant high school students. Some of my students characterized my delivery in the early years of teaching as similar to "somebody delivering a sermon." I think I managed quite well (though I will never be sure) to conceal my orientation until my last three years of teaching, when I'd grown old enough not to care anymore. Besides, my partner and I determined the classroom closet had taken—and was continuing to take—a tremendous toll on our relationship. In fact, the psychological consequences of years of lying to students, sidestepping honesty with colleagues (a much harder task), and experiencing rage at the effects of institutionalized repression contributed to the poisoning of fifteen years of commitment. Ironically, almost two years after I resigned from teaching, Robert and I broke up.

Yet preface never fully sets the stage for context, and none of what has preceded fully explains why I chose to write *Witness*. In reality, I do not now know in full. Since entering college in 1972, I have been a student of armchair theology, reading many books composed by religionists and theologians renowned in legitimate fields where I felt I never legitimately belonged. Always, my studies inspired fantasies of what Dann Hazel, the pastor, might have been had I not gotten cold feet, had I defied the status quo of Lutheran canon, had I worn the costume of pious leadership. Interwoven throughout the scripts of my fantasies was the sensation that something precious had been stolen from me. The bandits? The Religious Right, of course—a descriptive reference to leaders of conservative church traditions who, with missionary fervor and determination, attempt to coerce the American public into a belief that their religious views are the only ones with spiritual and redemptive validity.

As I crept from the comfort of my closet, I attended conferences, workshops, and services sponsored by fundamentalists who employ some of the most hate-filled and insulting rhetoric I have ever heard. Jesus is their weapon; fear is their tactic. War is the metaphor for their religion. Bringing God to a spiritually starving nation demands the vilification of gays and lesbians (and a few other groups, too) who, in their perception, stand in the way of God's great social plan to transform the United States into a New Canaan. Most mainline churches, although admittedly uncomfortable with gay and lesbian congregants and ministers, seldom use ecclesiastical power to translate prejudice into politics. At worst, mainline traditions hold their gay and lesbian congregants at arm's length, adopting a "welcoming but not affirming" stance. Increasingly, gays and lesbians join affirming denominations, like the United Church of Christ or the Unitarian Universalist Church, a nondoctrinal church whose origins lie in Christianity. Their ultimate move might be to join forces with the Universal Fellowship of Metropolitan Community Churches, which serves primarily gay and lesbian worshipers.

I have listened to Pat Robertson bash the "liberal scourge" during a Christian Coalition fund-raiser. As I rushed to an educators' conference, I pushed through crowds of Beverly LaHaye's Concerned Women for America, who condemn the homosexual agenda of "recruitment" in the public school system. And I have participated in a "love-in" response to Lou Sheldon as he reduced homosexual orientation solely to a behavior-based crime against nature brought about by inadequate parents. Once, I felt my faith was internal, truth-bound, and invincible; now, my faith has endured so many attacks that I have grown weary of the constant resistance. Maybe I had been wrong about God's love for me. Maybe Christianity—a religion I once regarded as the One and Only Way—was never the way for me. I *knew* my love for my spouse was just as strong, as noble, as God-given as any heterosexual's love for his or her spouse. But Christianity's most outspoken representatives were telling me that I had been misreading the truth all along. My love was nothing more than a parody of the only love that counts in God's eyes. Once, I was convinced of God's love for me. Christianity said God loves the sinner but hates the sin, yet how could that which makes me love so deeply be separated from the person God created? At this point in my spiritual growth—or spiritual repression, depending on one's point of view—I didn't even care. If Christians within repressive faith traditions didn't want to share Jesus—if Christ wasn't a savior of all people—then those so offensively certain of their chosen status could have Him. I would find another path to salvation and spiritual growth. Besides, my intellect had begun to equate Christianity to anti-intellectualism; I felt myself superior to it.

A few years ago, solely out of respect for my aging parents' wishes, I attended Sunday service with them at their church—once mine, too, for twenty-two years—while spending Father's Day weekend with them. As fate would have it, the same pastor who had encouraged me to enter the ministry—a man who relinquished the pulpit to accept an administrative position in the South Carolina synod of the Evangelical Lutheran Church in America (ELCA)—was substituting for St. Paul's regular pastor, who was vacationing in Virginia with his wife and two children. To one who believes in an interventionist God, his presence that Father's Day was no coincidence. Although I had never come out to this minister, he had always appeared to understand the turmoil I suffered while deciding whether to seek admission to the seminary. He had watched me closely and guided me. He helped me locate scholarship funds for my undergraduate studies. He had taken the time to talk with me about religious experiences that confused me still, years after having experienced them. He had helped me understand biblical exegesis by presenting theology in an informal, enjoyable atmosphere during catechism classes. I had noticed, on multiple occasions, his attentive eye—his eye on the sparrow. At that time, I felt vulnerable. I was convinced that he knew more about me than he would ever divulge or that I would divulge to him.

This Father's Day sermon strengthened my belief that I was right. The text of the sermon was the Book of Genesis (Chapter 2, verse 18): "It is not good that the man should be alone." Immediately, my gay defenses arose. Right away, I assumed that his sermon would be yet another treatise on the superiority of heterosexual love. But he surprised me. Although the congregation was particularly restless that warm June morning, my old pastor's eyes met mine and kept coming back to meet them, time and again, during the course of his sermon. I was struck by the unreasonable sensation that no one else was listening. They had heard all of this before, but why hadn't I? In a sense, he and I alone shared this sanctuary with its nineteenth-century ceiling constructed in the shape of the Cross. Behind and above me was a balcony where the slaves of wealthy farmers once sat, tight in their places and afraid to move.

As I glanced away from the balcony, used now only on special occasions for a brass ensemble to accompany the old Hammond organ, I remembered that a prevalent concern during the sixties among church council members was the possibility of African American worshipers infiltrating Sunday service.

"What can we do?" asked a distraught council member during the congregational meeting called specifically to address the church's response to the integration laws that would take effect in several days. No one understood whether the impact of this legislation would extend to the church community.

Although an adolescent then, I recall the question easily. It disturbed me, as a middle school student, and it disturbs me now. The pastor—a man who preceded my old pastor by one short, two-year term—instructed the council to question all dark faces who entered the church.

"Ask them why they are here," the pastor instructed. "If they say they are here to worship, then allow them inside. What else *can* we do, after all?" he added wearily, after a slight pause.

I remember that pastor's response now. I recognize the obvious parallel between what is happening in churches today and what happened in the sixties at St. Paul. Gay men and lesbians are interrogated, distrusted, and encouraged to remain among our "own kind," as though we belong to a different species with a genetic dispensation for herd behavior. What we express as genuine in our hearts is regarded by many Christians with suspicion, even hostility. What have we done to deserve this lack of respect, this marginalization? Who are we to have our faith diminished and scorned? Are we so slavish, so disempowered, that we must allow others to define us?

"You have your own neighborhoods, your own churches, even your own businesses." The church council actually *practiced* the words they would speak to the children of Africa. "Why do you want anything to do with mine? Why don't you admit it? You're here to cause trouble."

And yet, at the heart of the Christian message we find the idea of inclusiveness, the idea of unfolding God's growing message through an expanding church. Jesus' message was that all of us have value—to God, to each other, to ourselves. The church has room for an assortment of people. To be herded to the balcony denies our value, belittles our gifts and talents and diminishes our integrity. Arrogance replaces humility among those with seats downstairs. Unity bows to compartmentalization. Christianity is diminished in ways we cannot fully recognize—at least, not now, not at this particular juncture in its evolution.

The healing that began at St. Paul on Father's Day continued with yet another baptism—the conversations, soul-searching, and reading in which I engaged in preparation of this book. My mind, soul, and spirit were immersed for more than a year in the issues of sexual orientation and religion. Through numerous conversations with dozens of gay, lesbian, and straight ministers, I found new respect, both for my own spiritual growth and for the struggle occurring now in Christian faith communities. As I listened to their stories, I empathized with their feelings of isolation, exclusion, and pain. I felt my heart leap at their experiences of God's grace bestowed on them, despite and because of their sexual orientation. As I scheduled the last of my interviews, my old pastor's sermon pulled me back. It brought me a little closer to the God I understood.

"When God said it is not good for man to be alone," he said, his gaze settling on me, "He did not mean that every man, to be true to God's purpose, should marry a woman. That is not God's intent for every man. On this joyous Father's Day, we must take a renewed look at God's intent for us. It is up to each man in this congregation, whether he is a father or not, to determine his own way to combat the separation that is a major part of the human experience."

It was the first step—admittedly, a small step, but a significant one. I could not—cannot—shake his words from my heart. In fact, he opened my heart to the words of the ministers whose stories you find within these pages. The experiences and insights of these men and women provide comfort—and a commitment to learn more about this growing religion called Christianity. What does it really mean to those of us who are gay and lesbian? What does it mean to those, regardless of their sexual orientation, who continue to struggle with gay and lesbian issues? How does the clerical closet damage both the gay and lesbian clergy who remain there, and their congregations who hear God's message delivered from the shadows? How have honesty, affirmation, and celebration healed both gay and lesbian ministers and their congregations, as well as challenged faith communities to affirm gay and lesbian lives without risking destruction? How do the responses to gay and lesbian parishioners and ministers within faith traditions heighten—or diminish—the Christian's capacity to love?

Ultimately, my own learning continues through the words of clergy who spent many hours with me. Unknowingly, these men and women helped a man "who got cold feet" understand all over again.

1

THE SCHEME OF THINGS

Speaking the Truth Gradually

Ordained an Episcopal priest in 1983, Joseph Davis, who currently serves a parish in the Southwest, drifted from Christianity in his teens, though he remained keenly interested in spirituality. Even as a boy, he read works dealing with various eastern philosophies. "Then, when I was fifteen, I came in contact with an evangelical strand of Christianity," he relates. "I had, if not a conversion experience, then a recommitment to the Christian perspective. However, what was most influential for me was living with a group of evangelicals who lived communally on a four hundred-acre farm in Ohio. I spent the mornings in study and worked on the farm in the afternoon. At the young age of sixteen, it was a good formative experience for me."

Though Joseph knew at an early age that he was attracted to other boys, he didn't act on that knowledge for many years. "When I entered college, I was still convinced homosexuality was wrong," he says. "I dated women, but had no sexual outlet. By the end of my freshman year, I knew I wanted to enter the ministry. So, I made the changes in my course work to accommodate that decision. College was a safe place to be, and perhaps a safe place to hide from my sexual conflict."

Once Joseph finished college, he entered an evangelical seminary. "However, I was pretty convinced that I needed to look for something other than the American Baptist Convention in which I had been raised, though many members of my family were committed to that tradition," he says. "I made the change to the Episcopal Church. While attending the evangelical seminary, I became romantically involved with the woman who eventually became my wife. Ironically, during the same period of time I also began to change my theological views regarding homosexuality."

Despite his more positive regard of homosexual expression, Joseph stuck to his decision not to act on his homosexual impulses. "Had I not married, I would probably have been at a much different place in my life," he explains. "With varying degrees of discomfort, I negotiated my marriage for ten years."

However, his wife "came to understand herself as a lesbian and left the marriage. We had no children. My wife was disinclined for a variety of reasons." Right after their divorce, Joseph began to "claim my gay identity. I had made the journey toward intellectual reconciliation already. Certainly, as I broadened my vision of scripture, I read less fundamentalistically. I placed those passages [which are often cited to condemn homosexuality] in a historical context and understood them as subject to human development and new insights. I began to see the Bible as an unfolding of truth rather than a calcified vision of revelation."

One truth that unfolded dramatically before him was a clear vision of God's intent for human sexuality. "Mutual support is a human need that is met by the best of sexual expression and generativity," he explains. "This generativity can mean procreation in a literal way or in differing manners; a same-sex partnership can generate something greater, something that transcends the sum of its parts—and enables deep contribution beyond the relationship. Human growth occurs in healthy relationships assisted by mature reflection and a commitment to meet the world in contributive ways. In long-term relationships—and not just in heterosexual long-term relationships—there is often a substantive contribution to the solidity of culture and community."

Joseph believes that marriage rights should extend to gay and lesbian couples. "Monogamy is a highly-valued and worthy goal for both straight and gay people," he explains. "Our culture favors serial monogamy for straight people—the stance largely adopted in the gay and lesbian community as well. There is little difference between the ways homosexual and heterosexual people couple. Still, people need to test their vocation in relationships. Once you find a relationship with a strong foundation, there comes a time to think about an enduring and encumbering commitment to another person. I think the refusal to shoulder monogamous and exclusive relationships is perhaps for both straights and gays an unwillingness to take on the duties of self-sacrifice and encumbrance with a larger vision in mind. I find myself skeptical, therefore, about those legal half-measures offered through domestic partnerships. I think that, given the Constitution, it's inevitable that civil rights for homosexuals will be granted eventually. Those rights are more important to us, really, than religious marriage."

Despite such strong convictions about same-sex marriage and other gay and lesbian justice issues, Joseph has never "come out" to his congregation. "However, I don't present myself [to my parishioners] as other than what I am," he explains. "Neither am I overt in declaring myself to be gay. I'd say that 'don't-ask-don't-tell' prevails in my case. Most of my parishioners assume that I'm straight. Probably some have sufficient indication to construe that I'm gay." But Joseph reflects that, in the interest of individual parishioners who come to him for counseling, he has occasionally disclosed his orientation. "Recently, I counseled a couple having trouble in a long marriage that appeared heterosexual in nature," he explains. "However, the male had determined he was gay. It was only honest to be forthcoming about my own situation. In another instance, a young man was confused about his sexuality and disclosed that confusion to his mother. I asked her for permission to speak to him regarding my own sexuality—to offer him a positive role model. It was important to do that only with permission from his family. It became incumbent on me, in both situations, to self-reveal because it was important in a parishioner's journey. Coming out in overt or loud ways would be detrimental to congregational life. But as my life solidifies, I suspect that my sexual orientation will become increasingly known."

Does Joseph worry that parishioners privy to knowledge of his sexual orientation might inform the entire congregation? "Well, yes, I do have a concern about that," he admits. "And yet I try to act on principle—the principle that it would be ignoble to withhold that information when it might benefit their circumstances. So be it if they violated my confidence and told the congregation. Of course, I would prefer that it is not noised around."

The Episcopal Church USA's official ordination policy toward gay and lesbian ministers "is very hard to articulate at present. The Episcopal Church has forever ordained gay and lesbian clergy. It has knowingly done so for twenty-five years. But those bishops who have ordained open, out homosexuals have been subject to varying degrees of harassment." Fortunately, Joseph's bishop has asserted his willingness to ordain openly gay and lesbian ministers. "But overall, [whether you're ordained] depends on which diocese you're in. The Episcopal Church has not passed canon law opening the priesthood to homosexual persons in any direct way."

Because of no formal protection from his denomination, Joseph is careful regarding his ecclesiastical position. "That's necessary, I think, to maintain my position as a gay man," he says. "Gay men and lesbians are welcome in our church; we have signed a diocesan statement to that effect. But I try not to be heavy-handed when I preach about justice issues—of which homosexuality is a pertinent one. I'm careful not to preach my personal agenda." Joseph's church sponsors outreach advertisements to the gay and lesbian community. "In gay and lesbian publications, we run both an Easter ad and a Christmas ad. We join other welcoming congregations who also purchase ads in gay and lesbian publications at critical times of the year. We are an embracing faith community."

Another component of Joseph's life makes a low profile difficult—a partnership that has continued for more than three years. Even denominations that affirm gay and lesbian lives accept celibate gay men and lesbians more readily than those in committed relationships. "We don't live together, and since I live in the rectory, doing so would pose a problem," he explains. "He maintains his own place. Still, we spend a lot of time together. It simply would not play well if we were together in the rectory. The continuation of our partnership requires purchasing a house eventually, but we have not seen our way clear to do that yet. The situation will partially resolve by my moving out of the rectory—and that's certainly an active aspiration. It would be a wonderful plan, except for financial limitations. Right now, it's difficult to see from here to there."

Joseph's partner "understands the current difficulties in the church," he says. "And [any relationship with clergy must survive] the usual difficulties of too little time together and disrupted weekends. We experience the same stress of heterosexual marriages, though with many additional stressors. There is the difficulty of trying to conduct my personal life as something that is sundered from my work life. That, for me, is much more difficult than my partner realizes. I know—from having been married to a woman—how much parish life and personal life are interpenetrating. It's difficult not to be able to conduct a normal parish life, which would ordinarily integrate public face and private space. [Not being free to acknowledge my love for my partner] is the largest stressor I experience. It impacts my partner commensurately in this profoundly difficult area." Joseph's partner, although an Episcopalian, does not belong to Joseph's church. "It would be inappropriate to have a relationship with a parishioner," he says. "Besides, he's deeply committed elsewhere."

When working with other gay and lesbian Christians, Joseph encounters a great deal of suspicion—and sometimes, even hostility. "I've been active with the Log Cabin Republicans, where I've made many friends," he says. Log Cabin, the nation's largest gay and lesbian Republican organization, has fifty state chapters, a national office staff in Washington, D.C., and a federal political action committee (PAC) that raises one hundred thousand dollars per election cycle for Republican candidates. "I'm somewhat involved in the organization still, but I find myself less committed to the Republican Party because of that party's increasing social intolerance. And yet I cherish many economic values that the Republican Party advocates. Some friendships, both inside and outside this organization, were hard-won. There is much skepticism among church-damaged individuals within Log Cabin. Some gay men and lesbians hold me at arm's length because they think I'm insufficiently out or because of their suspicions regarding Christianity. I've encountered suspicion and hostility because of my position as a Christian priest who's not entirely out—or not as vocal as some judge I ought to be."

However, as Joseph meets other gays and lesbians through his ministry, he hopes they always experience his deepest respect regardless of their religious stance. "I often find that people aren't struggling so much with Christianity as they are with their families or culture at large. And although those are of importance to the church, gays and lesbians must see how the church can tangibly assist them with these concerns," he explains. "Some of the younger [gay and lesbian] people I've encountered—well, I've been impressed with their lack of pathology and their relative self-confidence. It indicates to me how many steps have been taken by the larger culture. Those young people are so well-adjusted that they are often beyond justifying homosexuality, looking instead to their religion for a deeper spirituality. They expect their religion to embrace their sexuality. I think we're seeing a paradigm shift among younger people. Conversely, in my pastoral ministry to straight people, there is a broad range of perspective. I think with a careful personal stance you can help people deepen their understanding. To my fundamentalist-oriented congregants who can't shake their fundamentalism regarding homosexuality, I'm outspoken, without being out. I'm consistent in what I say. [Fundamentalists] seem so fragile in their perspective. Many of them, at least, are open to growth, however slow."

Joseph admits discomfort in not having explicitly acknowledged his identity to his congregation. "But there is real value in being at the place I am," he says. "I am presently not an explicitly open gay man, but neither am I hidden or closeted. This twilight position serves my people well. It's extremely difficult to inhabit this gray area, but it allows my parishioners to encounter gay-friendly perspectives without throwing up all sorts of barriers because of unrealized prejudices they may have. I'm able to serve them well from this stance. However, it would probably be a disservice to the church to remain there indefinitely. I must become clearer in learning how to express to them the fullness of who I am. There is great value in having gay and lesbian clergy who transition slowly, bringing parishioners along a little at a time in this complex, nuanced world. I want to be respectful of the institution and people I serve. I don't want to be seen as someone who forces them to serve my particular needs. At the same time, the truth, I realize, makes you free. As I speak the truth gradually, my orientation will become clear to my parishioners. It will be freeing to me—and to the people I serve."

Why This Issue Now?

Joseph's willingness to relate to his parishioners from a "twilight position" reflects the stance of many closeted gay and lesbian ministers who know that, in coming out, they will either encounter full-fledged rejection from their faith tradition, or be thrust to the center of controversy. Ministers like Joseph perhaps live what Marcus Borg calls a "life of bondage" when, if permitted to witness to their faith honestly, they could live "life in the presence of God."[1] When Christians live in faith and full candor, their lives are opened to the possibility for greater transcendence.

However, those journeys of transcendence are influenced strategically by how one thinks of Jesus because how Christians think of Jesus is also how they think of the Christian life, says Elizabeth Clark, professor of theology at Duke University.[2] Unfortunately, as scholars in search of the historical Jesus attest, Christians in each era perceived Jesus in a way that suited their needs for the development of the church and the Christian religion at that particular time. In fact, every generation acts on an impulse to reinvent Jesus once again in order to understand him.

A singular appeal of Christianity to gay and lesbian Christians—and one reason so many refuse to give up the struggle for inclusion and affirmation—has always been the fact that the historical Jesus possessed an ability to attract a dedicated group of people who lived on society's fringes. "Why was the Christian community something that people wanted to join?" asks Helmut Koester, professor of New Testament Studies and Winn Professor of Ecclesiastical History at Harvard Divinity School. "Certain parts of the early Christian mission were intent in creating a new community. Only for that reason was this movement successful. . . . There is a future for the individual." Koester adds that the early Christian community was a very hospitable one for marginalized individuals. "Here is a community that invites you, which makes you an equal with all other members of that community. . . . Moreover, the commandment of love is decisive. That is, the care for each other becomes very important. People are taken out of an isolation. . . . Christianity really established a realm of mutual social support for the members who joined the church. So, Christianity could adjust itself to different types of people."[3]

The establishment of a moral climate within a given culture has always been the foremost goal of Christianity, according to Rodney Stark.[4] "Christianity taught that mercy is one of the primary virtues—that a merciful God requires humans to be merciful," writes Stark. "Moreover, the corollary that because God loves humanity, Christians may not please God unless they love one another was something entirely new. Perhaps even more revolutionary was the principle that Christian love and charity must extend beyond the boundaries of family and tribe, that it must extend to 'all those who in every place call on the name of our Lord Jesus Christ.'" Gay and lesbian Christians make strong demands on faith communities for acceptance on this basis. However, acculturated prejudices and certain troublesome scriptural passages often create major obstacles for inclusion, whether inclusion means inviting gay and lesbian parishioners into the faith community or accepting the leadership of gay and lesbian clergy.

Invariably, many Christians who readily condemn homosexuality often disregard other restrictions found in scripture. "Should we also follow the biblical tradition of promoting slavery (Leviticus 25:44–46; Ephesians 6:5), or the one of keeping the disabled from our places of worship (Leviticus 21:18–23)?" Duane Simolke asks.[5] "Should we bring back the death penalty for people who use God's name in vain (Leviticus 24:16), anyone who commits adultery (Leviticus 20:10), a woman who loses her virginity before marriage (Deuteronomy 22:13–21), a son who acts stubbornly or rebelliously (Deuteronomy 21:18–21), and 'everyone who curses his father or his mother' (Leviticus 20:9)? Too many people scream verses that condemn others, but find ways to disregard verses that condemn themselves."

Simolke reminds his readers that Jesus' message was one of love and acceptance, not condemnation. "Though living in the openly bisexual Roman culture, Christ never mentioned same-gender relations; instead, he taught people about love and acceptance, even going out of his way to meet the rejected half-breeds of Samaria," he continues. "Yes, he mentioned heterosexual relationships, but he never condemned gay ones. His only possible reaction to homosexuality occurred when he healed the 'pais' of a centurion (Matthew 8:5–13). Though translators render it 'servant,' the word *pais* also carried gay connotations at that time—a connotation strengthened by the obvious love between this particular centurion and his servant. Christ reacted to the centurion's love by healing the servant. Notice, however, that Christ made no judgment of his relationship."

In fact, according to Mike Silverman, the Bible never condemned homosexuality.[6] "When you go to a bookstore and buy a Bible today, you are getting the product of many centuries of translation," Silverman writes. "The Bible was originally written in Greek, Hebrew, and Aramaic. It was then translated into Latin, and across the centuries, finally, into Old English, and then today, into Modern English. If you have ever played the game, 'Telephone,' you have an idea of what all this translation can do to the original meaning of something." All that can be said about the Bible's stance toward homosexuality, Silverman says, is that "it bans homosexual behavior for Jewish priests following a four thousand-year-old version of their religion in the days of animal sacrifice and living surrounded by idol-worshiping hostile tribes."

The current debates within faith communities over issues of homosexuality center around the nature of "settled truth," according to Peter Gomes, preacher to Harvard University.[7] "All aversion to homosexuality is biblically-based," he writes. "No language had a word for homosexual before the late nineteenth century. You would not have found the word in any Bible in any language before 1946. Paul did not discuss gay persons, but only homosexual acts committed by heterosexual persons. What is unnatural is the one behaving after the manner of the other."

The Bible and Homosexuality, a four-part study by John M. House, pastor of Body of Christ Church in Fort Lauderdale, Florida, illuminates the dangers of literalism in biblical interpretation.[8] "It's much more important to understand the message of scripture as opposed to some pointless debate such as whether God actually created the earth in seven twenty-four-hour periods," says House, who served Southern Baptist churches until 1985, when he disassociated from the Southern Baptist Convention because his orientation was perceived as an impediment to ministry. "When Christians spend more time debating the 'inerrancy' of scripture than they do telling others about the forgiving love of Jesus Christ, then, quite simply, they're sinning. They turn the scripture into an idol that keeps them from the mission of Christ."

Meticulously, House analyzes Bible passages traditionally used to condemn homosexuality. "The Bible refers to Sodom and Gomorrah many times," he continues. "In Isaiah, Chapter One, the prophet refers to Sodomites as murderers, idolaters, oppressors, rebels and thieves, but never once as homosexuals. Jesus referred to Sodom's sin as one of inhospitality or rejecting God (Luke 10). Never once did he mention homosexuality."

So why do many church leaders—particularly in conservative traditions—often allude to the Sodom passages as indictments of homosexuality? "Flavius Josephus was a Jew who lived from A.D. 37 to about A.D. 100," House explains. "He was very well educated and wrote many works about Jewish history. He is considered by many scholars to be the leading contributor to information concerning the Hebrews from some source other than the Bible. In his book, *The Antiquities of the Jews,* which reads almost like the Bible, Josephus injects sexual overtones into the Sodom and Gomorrah story. This was no doubt directly related to his time spent with the Romans who thought nothing of raping an enemy defeated in battle. . . . Research indicates that Josephus' writing is the first time sexuality was implied in the Genesis account almost twenty-two hundred years after Sodom was destroyed. Yet, oddly enough, it has remained the prevailing thought to this day."

In his study, House clarifies the role of the Levitical laws in ancient Judaism—laws that make the strongest statements against male homosexual practices (Leviticus 18:22 and 20:13). "Several cultural factors must be taken into account when considering the extent to which any Levitical edicts apply to us today," House says. "The larger a people's population, the stronger they were. Israel was constantly at war. As a result, their population [continued to be depleted]. This put great emphasis on reproduction. Two men or two women cannot reproduce. Besides, the Hebrews lacked a cultural concept of homosexuality as a sexual orientation. It was unimaginable to the Levitical writer that sexual activity between two people of the same gender could exist as an expression of love. Nearly all homosexual activity the Hebrews saw was that of temple prostitutes or anal rapists. These were considered the only modes by which a man would 'lie with a man as one lies with a woman.' This argument is further supported by the fact that lesbianism is condemned nowhere in Leviticus or any of the Old Testament."

Marcus Borg perceives the implication of one of Paul's most oft-quoted messages to include gay men and lesbians. "It seems to me that the shattering of purity boundaries by both Jesus and Paul should also apply to the purity code's perception of homosexuality," Borg writes. "Homosexual behavior should therefore be evaluated by the same criteria as heterosexual behavior. It also seems to me that the passage in which Paul negates the other central polarities of his world also means, 'In Christ, there is neither straight nor gay.'"[9]

A number of other factors, besides scriptural interpretation, influence the controversies over sexual orientation issues occurring at this point in the history of Christianity. Because of the heightened visibility of gay and lesbian

Americans who are calling on society to atone for perceived injustices committed against them, heterosexual Americans have begun to examine their own attitudes—attitudes that are reflected in, shaped, and sometimes exploited by all faith communities. A national News Odyssey poll of 752 adults revealed that most Americans—with the exception of some evangelical groups—want a hands-off approach by faith groups when it comes to the controversial issue of homosexuality. Although a near-majority believes homosexuality is morally wrong (47 percent) and a homosexual relationship is not equivalent to a heterosexual relationship in the eyes of God (60 percent), straight Americans do not want their religious groups supporting attempts to change homosexuals into heterosexuals through ex-gay ministries (66 percent). They also do not want their churches to take formal positions on the issue of homosexual rights (59 percent). Although the majority of Americans would welcome homosexuals as church members (54 percent), they oppose ordaining gay and lesbian clergy and instituting rituals to bless gay marriages (64 and 69 percent, respectively). And whatever reservations heterosexual Americans may have about homosexuality, most of them do not worry that homosexual people are trying to recruit others to their "lifestyle" (72 percent).[10]

For the past thirty years, the frequency with which denominations have had to deal directly with the issue of homosexuality—and with gay and lesbian parishioners and clergy—has increased tremendously because growing numbers of gay men and lesbians keep coming out. Unfortunately, debates within church assemblies "have produced more heat than light," according to staff writer Clark Morphew (*St. Paul Pioneer Press,* November 29, 1997). "No Protestant denomination has resolved the issue to all of its constituents' satisfaction." In fact, most faith communities expect their ordained ministers "who are homosexual in their self-understanding . . . to abstain from homosexual sexual relationships." However, increasing numbers of gay and lesbian ministers—"many people with unique gifts"—feel such a restriction to be unfair and unreasonable, particularly when their partnerships adhere to patterns of monogamy, commitment, and integrity, similar aspirations in heterosexual marriages.

A few denominations—like the United Church of Christ (UCC), the Universal Fellowship of Metropolitan Community Churches (MCC), and the Unitarian Universalist Association (UUA)—ordain gay and lesbian clergy, including those who are involved in committed, monogamous relationships. "On the whole, the UCC works from a basis of belief in fidelity in covenanted relationships and integrity in singleness," Rev. David McMahill told Morphew. "Now integrity—that's a very broad word. We do not encourage promiscuity, clearly. We're not saying that in our recognition of gay or lesbian partnerships that anything goes."

"The battles over homosexuality also tap into deeper theological questions that are very much in play at the end of the second millennium," writes

Steve Kloehn ("Heated Debate on Homosexuality Just a Beginning," *Chicago Tribune*, March 20, 1998). "The first question is about the proper approach to Scripture, which most Protestants agree is the source of religious authority on earth. Simply acknowledging that authority, however, does not explain how to approach the texts, how to reconcile them with conscience and modern culture, or how to understand their apparent contradictions. The second is about the authority of the church—where it comes from, where it sits and how it stacks up against personal belief."

Understanding and interpretation are problematic in the "religious civil war" that rages in faith communities, says religion editor James D. Davis ("Can We Live Together as a Church?" *Fort Lauderdale Sun-Sentinel*, June 14, 1998). Part of the shift from silence into debate has been "in reading the Bible in the tribal context from which it sprang," Lesley Northup, assistant professor of religious studies at Florida International University, told Davis. "Individual identity was not a problem with the ancient world—you simply did what was best for the tribe. Now we're less prone to throw people away because of categories."

Why are gays and lesbians interested in joining faith communities that have historically condemned them? "AIDS has aged [gays and lesbians] tremendously," Rev. Deborah L. Johnson, founder of Inner Light Ministries in Aptos, California, told Rhonda Smith (*The Washington Blade*, December 26, 1997). "Because of that, we have come to a greater understanding of our spirituality, and we're much more willing now to demand the dignity that spirituality affords us." Furthermore, the public and personal process of "coming out" brings with it a gradual redefinition of self, accompanied by emotional and spiritual growth.

However, the desire for inclusion in mainline denominations is not unanimous among gay men and lesbians for reasons that are not difficult to understand. "Religion has been a very primal and painful source for a lot of gay [and lesbian] people," Dr. Jeanne Knepper, director of Affirmation: United Methodists for Lesbian, Gay and Bisexual Concerns, told Smith. "It's like the very mouthpiece of God has been telling them they are wrong and perverted. So, it's entirely appropriate for lots of people to be very suspicious of anyone who comes to them and says, 'I'm religious.' Because then, the question becomes, 'What do you want me to give up in my life?'"

Because the path of Christianity, throughout history, has frequently led to suffering, exclusion, and exploitation within marginalized faith communities, the question is not without merit. "Christians have always carried the unshakable premise that everyone should be a Christian, and the only way to salvation is through the figure of Jesus Christ," writes Anthony Colman (*Daily Nebraskan*, January 28, 1998). "This narrow vision of faith and moral life has created an obsession with good and evil, and defined what is morally good as singularly the province of Christians. Behind this version of Christian faith lies the actual belief system and practice with a rather complicated existence." Some faith communities justified a number of "vices" on the basis of certain biblical passages. "If Christianity can be implicated in the unjust practices of slavery, as an oppositional force against women's basic rights, and now against the basic rights of gay and lesbian persons, why should we accept this structure of faith as legitimate and moral?"

But many churches are trying to correct what they perceive to be injustices of the past. Some clearly welcome gay and lesbian parishioners with open arms. "[These churches] have been struggling internally for several years [over] the ordination of sexually active gay men and lesbians and the performing of so-called covenant ceremonies for homosexual couples," writes Benjamin Hubbard (*Los Angeles Times,* June 6, 1998). "These are difficult and divisive issues for liberal Protestant churches in particular, whose memberships have declined significantly in the past quarter century. But these churches need to send strong, unequivocal messages condemning all forms of hateful speech and actions against gays and lesbians, and to become more accepting of and welcoming to persons of all sexual orientations. Some churches have done so, but they are in the minority."

Acceptance of gay and lesbian parishioners and pastors does not mean abandoning morality—a distinction often lost on heterosexual parishioners with deep fears and prejudices or a literal mindset in their approach to scriptural interpretation. "To be moral, progressive churches say, sexual relationships must be loving, faithful, thoughtful and between equals," writes Dana Sterling (*Tulsa World,* June 21, 1998). "Under those rules, gay relationships can be just as moral as heterosexual marriages. On the other hand, promiscuity, exploitation, violence, and abuse of children are always immoral, whether they occur in gay or straight relationships."

But when parishioners balk at the idea of accepting gays and lesbians as either fellow worshippers or as their ministers, the blame is often placed on the influence of media-glorified Religious Right rhetoric. "Gays and lesbians do not threaten you," writes David Cheezem (*Anchorage Daily News,* March 18, 1998). "The real threat to your moral foundation is in the smiley-face fascism of the religious right. Their hatred is not righteous. Don't get sucked in."

Many mainline Christians resent the accusation of being unduly influenced by fundamentalism. Homosexuality is a difficult issue for them, their faith notwithstanding. Several factors define the latest wave of antigay sentiment, according to Elsa C. Arnett and Lydia Martin (*Miami Herald,* April 21, 1998). "First, there has been a return to more conservative values, reflected in part by a falling in divorce rate and a drop in out-of-wedlock birth rates," they write. "Also, many people don't believe sexual orientation should be accorded the same rights as skin color and gender. In fact, polls show that while most Americans think gays should not be discriminated against on the job, more than two-thirds don't think they need such rights as marriage. All of this might seem surprising because it's happening at a time when gays [and lesbians] appear to be winning public acceptance and gaining political clout."

Many churches protest that they *will* embrace gay and lesbian worshippers—as long as they are willing to change. If, in God, all things are possible, then, according to the beliefs of many Christians, faith in Christ can effect transformation into heterosexuality. "[But that's] very much like trying to change people who were left-handed," Rev. Glenna Shepherd told the *Atlanta Journal-Constitution* (June 6, 1998). "In centuries past, that was someone who was born of the devil. Now we have learned that that's how their brains worked. They were born that way."

But no consensus exists among church leadership that gays and lesbians are "born that way." Leaders on both sides of the controversy see themselves in a battle for the "soul of the church," according to Gayle White (*Atlanta Journal-Constitution,* June 7, 1998). "The question is whether the country's historic Christian bodies can hold together while the grappling goes on."

The grappling often gets fierce. Gays and lesbians reject the inference of many churches that they have a treatable illness or a genetic defect—like alcoholism or a gambling addiction. Rev. Bob Kuyper, founder of the United Methodist Church's Transforming Congregations movement, which accepts gay and lesbian parishioners who express desire to "switch" to heterosexuality, contends that behaviors don't have to be accepted just because they are biologically rooted (Lisa Millegan, *Modesto Bee,* June 28, 1998). But Kuyper's position offends gays and lesbians who have traveled a hard road toward self-acceptance. The offense is also felt by gay and lesbian Christians who perceive their sexual orientation as a gift from God. They experience relationships that are just as wholesome, as loving, as permanent as the best of heterosexual marriages, they say.

Kuyper's perspective is growing increasingly offensive to straight Christians, too. Dr. Beverly Dale, Executive Director of the Christian Association at the University of Pennsylvania, writes of her escape from heterosexuality's closet into a new realization about sexual orientation ("Straight Folks Have Closets, Too," *The Daily Pennsylvanian,* October 22, 1996). "Being gay is being able to love someone of the same sex to a greater depth than a member of the opposite sex," writes Dale, who believes that "God always revises our boundaries outward. . . . Being gay is a matter of love, not sex. Being gay is who a person is—*not* what he or she does. Being gay is part of the individual, not a separate entity. Living a lie is the 'sin,' not the fact that you are gay. If being gay were a choice, there would be no gays."

A large influence on Dale's "coming out" as a heterosexual ally was listening to Dr. Shirley M. Hunter, a counselor in Oklahoma City. "We cannot change being gay," she told Dale, "but we can live with the fact that we are. Being gay is accepting yourself—even when others do not accept you. You do not have to understand being gay to be gay. It is who you are. When not at war with the outside world, being gay is gentleness, warmth, and sensitivity. Being gay is being different, not 'bad,' even though we may be ridiculed about something we cannot change. Being gay is reaching that stage in life where we wonder why we spent so much time trying to gain acceptance from people who don't know or understand us. Being gay is who we are—and *nothing* in the world is more important than that."

Once gay and lesbian Christians reach that level of self-acceptance and self-affirmation, they recognize a personal, spiritual truth that often balkanizes faith communities. In their view, they are God's creation, too, and churches are wrong when they demand shame, dishonesty, or repentance.

Jesus Was So Mad About Us

Bob Jones University, located in Greenville, South Carolina, is arguably the most fundamentalist of all Bible schools in the United States. Yet Rev. Bob Arthur, an Omaha, Nebraska, resident who is also the coordinator for the Mountains and Plains District of the Metropolitan Community Church, not only attended school there, he also served as assistant dean of men for six years. "Homosexuality was not talked about a whole lot," he says. "The school also had the six-inch rule. There had to be at least six inches between you and a member of the opposite sex." Even today, interracial dating is forbidden on the Bob Jones' campus, nor are openly gay and lesbian alumni welcome to visit. "During my affiliation with the university, people who were caught in homosexual activity were sent home. As disciplinarian, I expelled ten or eleven men for that—but then, I had no concept of who I was at the time."

In 1971, Bob left his position at Bob Jones University a married man; in fact, by that time, he and his wife had been married for five years. "We moved to Massachusetts, where I worked as a police officer," he says. "During that time, I began to struggle with who I was. I realized I would have to break the news to my wife."

Not long after, an argument between Bob and his wife escalated into a confrontation of honesty.

"We never spend any time together," she complained. "Why *is* that?"

"Sometimes, I think I'm queer," Bob retorted. "Maybe that's why I avoid spending time with you."

She looked at him suspiciously. "You're kidding, right?"

Bob looked away, then shook his head.

"Well, so am I."

"Both of us had been running around, frantically trying to hide literature that would disclose our sexual orientation," Bob laughs. "Now, we're the best of friends. In fact, we see each other at least once a year."

Despite the undergirding of the university's fundamentalist philosophies,

Bob's studies gave him the tools to discover "the truth" about the Bible's stance on homosexuality. "There isn't any condemnation [of us] in the scripture," he explains. "Sometimes, the condemnation that's thrown our way comes from mistranslation. Other times, passages are taken out of context. What those passages speak of is the sin of making sex into God and putting it in front of the true God. They also address misusing or abusing other people. But the Bible doesn't speak at all of gay relationships. In fact, there are positive passages about the centurion and his servant—and of course, about David and Jonathan."

To the argument that gays and lesbians can change their orientation, Bob offers his own story in counterpoint. "I had totally sublimated my sexuality when I entered Bob Jones University," he says. "There, I realized I needed to get married if I was going to be a preacher. I decided to marry the only woman I was close to."

In fact, his wife's fiancé was Bob's best friend. "They had a number of fights and arguments," Bob continues. "Finally, they broke up. She was the only woman I allowed myself to get close to. We lived together for seven years. There was some sexual intimacy in that relationship; it was not frequent, but it was there."

Bob criticizes the smugness of ex-gay ministries when an occasional client announces his ability to function heterosexually. In such cases, Bob believes, functionality belies identity. "I have never met a true ex-gay," Bob says. "I'm convinced that we're born homosexual. It may take a while to discover our orientation. I don't deny that. I've had experiences with two individuals who have since gone 'ex-gay.' One affair lasted for a year or two. He was living a lie; finally, he returned to the gay community. Joe Dallas, founder of Genesis Counseling, an ex-gay ministry in Orange, California, was the other one; he and I were an item for a time. He is the only gay man I know who stayed with the movement for any length of time. He will not see or talk with me now. A number of organizations have tried to get us in the same room for a debate, but Joe resists those efforts."

Within the Metropolitan Community Church, Bob says, "we view sexuality as a God-given blessing. It is a major, important force in people's lives. We freely admit in our church that sexuality is an awareness through which we see what God has shown us. I recognize that many people think that what we're all about is homosexuality. But from day one, we bristled at being called a gay church. We were founded to provide ministry for people who felt rejected. It's not exclusive to the gay and lesbian community. Our churches have nongay people who are an essential part of our fabric. We attract divorcees, people with children who are gay and lesbian, and gay and lesbian parents."

Even so, gays and lesbians comprise the bulk of MCC membership; they can no longer tolerate a Christianity that has been so mean-spirited. "But even those denominations [that have been mean-spirited] are progressing,"

Bob says. "However, mainline churches move like molasses in January. It's telling that they are presently willing to discuss the issues; often, the voting around issues of inclusion is narrow. Those kinds of 'close calls' wouldn't have happened several years ago. And increasingly, mainline churches are willing to have fellowship with churches such as ours. That says a lot about the future of mainline denominations."

Father Jerry Sanders grew up in a small New England town that was over-whelmingly Roman Catholic—a tradition that has long informed gay and lesbian Christians that God loves them, even as it encourages them not to yield to "homosexual temptations." For homosexual Christians, celibacy is next to godliness. "I didn't even know about the existence of homosexuality until I started undergraduate school," Jerry says. "Actually, I came out while I was in the seminary. I did a lot of thinking and reading."

Jerry has been an ordained priest for more than thirteen years; he believes the Pope's position that homosexuality is an intrinsic moral evil is dead wrong. "He's grasping at straws," he says. "The Vatican is despairing of keeping the American church in order. Many of its edicts have simply been ignored by people in general—even by bishops. Besides, there's really a lot of room to play with how you approach the issues of homosexuality. Another thing that's interesting in the Catholic Church is the discrepancy between what we teach as the ideal on the one hand, as opposed to how you deal with these issues pastorally. It would be foolhardy to preach in your congregation against some of these controversial issues—like homosexuality and abortion, to name two. You'd lose some of your parishioners. However, how you deal with individuals—and their consciences after the fact—is quite a different thing."

Considering Catholicism's stance on human sexuality, it would be foolhardy for Jerry to come out to his congregation—if he intends to remain in the priesthood. "Certainly there are people around here who know I'm gay," he says. "And I think I would tell my parishioners—if I *had* to tell. One of the people I most admired died of AIDS a couple of years ago. His parish had previously been very homophobic. His sickness and subsequent death caused a lot of people to reevaluate their attitudes about a lot of things. Sure, it's unfortunate this gay priest's death had to happen. But it's an example of good growing out of the bad."

Despite his closeted status, Jerry speaks often from the pulpit about oppression and justice issues. "I might use gay and lesbian people in a list of groups who find themselves victims of oppression," he explains. "However, one crucial part of my ministry is networking with other clergy friends. One Episcopal priest, for example, is in some shit because her authorities support the mission of Exodus, the ex-gay ministry. Her whole diocese has put her through the ringer. Regarding the issue of coming out, my perception is that it's very important to retain ministers, even if they can't come out, who may have talents to help others make important strides. Relinquishing their ordination would accomplish little. Some of us must remain part of the system. Not all of us can pack our bags and move to the MCC."

Jerry does not recognize MCC's value, nor does he respect its mission. He regards MCC as a distraction from efforts that could go into changing attitudes within mainline denominations and the Catholic Church. "The MCC is one of the biggest personality cults I've ever seen," he says bluntly. "Each time founder Troy Perry rides in one of his limousines on Pride Day, it's like Jesus coming into Jerusalem. They play at church. They're dreadful people—and incredibly naïve to leave us adrift in the mainline churches. To leave because you don't like the way Mummy runs things is just awful. MCC infuriates me!"

Often, churches welcome gay and lesbian Christians, as long as they remain celibate and single. However, Jerry rejects the idea that gay and lesbian couples are incapable of committing to long-term relationships—or that it is a sin if they do. "I know successful couples who have been together for twenty or thirty years," he says. Jerry himself has been in a committed relationship for four years—a situation of which his congregation remains unaware. "Now, we don't live together," he explains. "I would personally have no problem with our living together—and *maybe* no one else would either. But he's in graduate school now. His studies require him to be a hundred miles away from Decatur [Georgia]. Still, ours is a strange and wonderful relationship. We're not sure what the circumstances of our lives will become. I don't even know whether I will continue to live in the Atlanta area. I'm neurotic about what's going to happen—not anxious, but not clear about it, either. But whatever happens, we will always be profoundly close to one another. It's very much a spiritual thing. It's an unusual respect we have for each other."

However, Jerry does not support the position favoring same-sex marriage. "It's not marriage, it can't be marriage, and I don't want it to be marriage," he says. "And I don't like the term 'holy union" either. It sounds like picking sides during some kind of civil war. But we have a need and a responsibility to help people stabilize and celebrate and acknowledge their relationships. As far as benefits are concerned, gay and lesbian partners should be entitled to exactly the same ones as heterosexual spouses—no more, no less."

Besides, if gay and lesbian unions were called something other than marriages, "the silly fear that many heterosexuals have would dissipate. But despite my position, the outrage that has been expressed against same-sex marriage is such a colossal display of stupidity and dumb homophobia. I can respect 'smart homophobia.' But the bottom line is that we need to sanction our relationships—whatever we call them."

In Jerry's mind, that sanction should include church recognition of gay and lesbian partnerships because "God has made a wide variety of people in his likeness," Jerry explains. "There is a variety of possibilities. I don't think God has problems with nearly as many things as humans do. God and Christ were so busy going about the business of loving us, and about the business of Jesus' coming. I don't see Jesus as a fix-it man—someone to 'fix' original sin. It was because of God's overwhelming love for humanity that he couldn't stay out of our flesh. He was so mad about us. Jesus was very hesitant to condemn anything God made, and wouldn't that include his gay and lesbian children? My experience was that I was born gay. Nothing necessarily 'put' me in that category. And I presume I am made in the image of God. I cannot think but that I'm okay."

When Jerry hears antigay rhetoric, he wants to "get down on my hands and knees and write in the dust on the floor God's two great commandments: love thy neighbor as thyself, and love God with all your heart. But people pick and choose the things they like, don't they? They pick what they hate. You can't take the whole issue of fundamentalism seriously or you'd go crazy. Living here in Decatur feels like I've walked through a hole into 1945—and into a very bad Faulkner novel."

Within the past decade, characters who would comfortably fit into a Faulknerian plot have emerged from quiet ministries onto center stage of a controversy that just won't go away.

What Makes a Person Christian?

In 1997, more than two hundred churches ordered the Hell House Kit, "the Christian Alternative to a Halloween Haunted House," from the Abundant Life Christian Center in Arvada, Colorado. Once the sets are erected, usually in church assembly halls, the costumes fitted, and the music filtered through the sound system, church members lead paying visitors through various scenes, including the tableau of a gay man's funeral, a simulated abortion, and a teen suicide. The scenes are designed to shock people out of their "sinful" behavior (*San Francisco Chronicle,* October 28, 1997).

"Successful fund-raising [by and for the Religious Right]," writes Betty McCollister ("Coming Soon to a Nearby City: God's Wrath," *The Daily Iowan,* June 18, 1998), "as any experienced practitioner will tell you, is most effective when it spreads fear, loathing and paranoia. For decades, these sentiments were aimed mostly at 'godless atheist commies.' To fill the vacuum left when communism went under, the Christian right intensified its vitriol against other targets, among them atheists, secular humanists, feminists, pro-choice advocates and homosexuals. Somehow, whether by accident or design, homosexuals now head the hate list."

Christian mainliners often resist any effort to lump their beliefs in the same category with those of fundamentalist Christians. Their objections to issues of homosexuality, they assert, are based on reason and rationality, not on the kind of visceral reaction of those who interpret the scripture literally. ("Homosexuality makes God vomit," Jay Grimstead, founder of the Coalition on

Revival, told McCollister.) However, though mainline faith communities don't accept—and are often embarrassed by—the extremism of the Religious Right, many ministers and parishioners assert that the right-wing media campaign against homosexuality has influenced the controversy currently being waged in mainline denominations.

James Dobson, the force behind Focus on the Family, a radio-based, conservative Christian ministry established in 1977, "portrays himself as a simple family man whose sole concern is to serve God and strengthen society's most basic institution," writes Christopher Ott.[11] His insistence that homosexuality has the capacity to topple families has made Dobson a particularly vocal agent against the gay and lesbian fight for justice and equal rights.

However, according to Ott, Dobson's now estranged cofounder, Gil Alexander-Moegerle, criticizes the existence of a "cultlike worship of Jim. I think the kindest thing you can say about Dobson's politics is that he's very ignorant. It is also accurate, though, to say that he is mean-spirited, divisive and intolerant. I think 'megalomaniac' is not too strong a word to use." Two occurrences contributed to the estrangement of the two men. First, Dobson objected to a marriage counseling session for Alexander-Moegerle and his wife that Dobson did not conduct. He thought his cofounder's choice of another counselor might erode Dobson's credibility, should the media make the discovery. Second, Dobson's refusal to allow his radio show to feature Christians who disagreed with Focus on the Family antagonized Alexander-Moegerle. "James Dobson clearly has tapped into the fears of his people," Ott writes. "They're afraid for their families—they're afraid for themselves—in a world filled with Darwinists, Sodomites and Disney characters, but also filled with less imaginary dangers like violence, cultural and economic changes and spiritual cynicism. He's turned that unease into a media empire. Increasingly, he is heeded by conservative politicians, and he is held in esteem by millions of American voters."

Jay Alan Sekulow, chief counsel of the American Center for Law and Justice, a legal arm of the Christian Coalition, says it is time to turn back the runaway train of homosexuality.[12] "If these [homosexual] extremists have their way, America will not only condone homosexuality, but will become the world's greatest promoter of every form of sexual deviancy," Sekulow writes. "The traditional family will be left in ruins and moral constraints will be cast aside—all under the guise of equality. If you look around, you can see that this is already happening. The train is approaching."

Sekulow points to the same-sex marriage issue as an example of the fast-approaching train. "If same-sex marriage is [ever] allowed, the family would never be the same," he writes. "America's moral landscape would be transformed, literally, overnight. That is why the same-sex marriage issue . . . is undoubtedly the most crucial battleground in today's culture war. In fact, it could be the decisive battle for the soul of America."

Many conservative Christians, like Donald E. Wildmon, founder of the American Family Association (AFA), never dreamed they "would see the day when sodomy would be called normal, and those who held to traditional values based on Christian teaching would be called bigots. . . . During the lifetime of the AFA, the movement to normalize homosexual behavior has exploded on the American scene"—a movement that must be resisted. Several principles should guide such resistance, one of which is that "the root of homosexuality is a sinful heart. It is the duty of individual Christians and Christ's Church corporately to bring the gospel to homosexuals and to speak out against the acceptance of sin in our culture. We oppose the gay movement's efforts to convince our society that their behavior is normal because we fear the judgment of God on our nation. [Besides], the gay movement is a progressive outgrowth of the sexual revolution of the past forty years and will lead to the normalization of even more deviant behavior."[13]

In a speech presented at Harvard University as part of the Third Annual National Coming Out of Homosexuality Day (October 10, 1997), Robert H. Knight, Director of Cultural Studies at the Family Research Council, told the crowd: "Nobody has to be gay. All the sham studies, propaganda from homosexual activists and media distortions cannot hide the truth. Men and women are different. Their bodies and minds were designed to complement each other. Homosexual behavior is a misuse of sexuality that has tragic consequences for individuals, families and communities. [And] as the so-called gay rights movement advances, other citizens are losing the freedom to disagree with it."

Knight cautioned his audience that same-sex marriage could lead to reprehensible and irreversible consequences. "Once the 'one-man, one-woman' definition is abandoned, there is no logical reason for limiting it to two people—or even to people," he says. "[And] why not have three partners? Or why not a man and his daughter? Or a man and his dog? The logical reason to extend 'marriage' to homosexual couples has nothing to do with marital integrity, but only reflects the fact that homosexuals want the same status regardless of its real meaning. Anything less, they say, is a denial of human rights . . . [But] destroying definitions does enormous damage not only to marriage, but to the idea of truth. Calling [the union of] two lesbians a 'marriage' is telling a lie, and official recognition of this lie breeds the sort of cynicism found in totalitarian societies, where lies are common currency."

In 1996, the American Family Association published *Homosexuality in America: Exposing the Myths* to combat "the destructive effects of homosexuality socially and personally"—a goal that can be accomplished only by facing the reality, understanding the agenda, and answering the arguments. The twenty-four-page booklet was widely distributed and posted on the organization's Web site. "We don't have to look at the vast spans of history to know that the contemporary state of decay in America and the breakdown of the family is due, at least in part, to the presence of homosexuality," Richard Howe states in the Introduction. In fact, the expansion of gay and lesbian "rights" is at least partially responsible for declining marriage rates and divorce rates—"especially among younger couples. Clearly," Howe continues, "the movement seeks not only tolerance for their lifestyle, but endorsement."[14]

Howe says he supports any special interest group—including homosexuals—seeking to "affect society in the way it perceives to be in its own best interest. Our quarrel with the homosexual movement is not at that level. Our argument is that to the degree that the homosexual movement changes society in its favor, (1) it will inevitably lead to an improper violation of the moral and religious sentiments of millions of Americans who oppose homosexuality, and (2) it will contribute to the overall decay of society. . . . Hopefully, it is not too late to rescue America from total moral collapse."

After "exposing the decadence of the homosexual lifestyle," the report addresses two issues that "should be important to Christians everywhere." First, "there is the concern about how we can forestall the further advance of the homosexual agenda. Second, there is the concern about what we can do for homosexuals themselves."

Responding to those concerns from a conservative scholarly perspective is the Ramsey Colloquium, a group of Jewish and Christian theologians, ethicists, philosophers, and scholars who consider questions on morality, religion, and public life.[15] Though the Ramsey Colloquium's report on homosexuality sounds compassionate and reasonable, its conclusions do not differ dramatically from those drawn by fundamentalists whose rhetoric frames the issues more flamboyantly. "Our statement is directed chiefly to debates over public policy and what should be socially normative," the report states. "We share the uneasiness of most Americans with the proposals advanced by the gay and lesbian movement."

Gay and lesbian people endorse a way of life that "accepts and encourages sexual relations for pleasure or personal satisfaction," the report continues. However, gay men and lesbians involved in committed long-term relationships would likely challenge the idea that their long-term partnerships flourish solely for the convenience of sex-on-demand. But the report incriminates homosexuality even more. "Permissive abortion, widespread adultery, easy divorce, radical feminism, and the gay and lesbian movement have not by accident appeared at the same historical moment. They have in common a declared desire for liberation from constraint—especially constraints associated with an allegedly oppressive culture and religious tradition. They also have in common the presuppositions that the body is little more than an instrument for the fulfillment of desire, and that the fulfillment of desire is the essence of the self."

For three decades, the conservative strand in American Christianity has offered what it considers a compassionate response to the problem of "homosexual bondage." However, at no earlier time in its history has the anti-homosexual movement surfaced with the impact of its 1998 campaign, when several right-wing organizations and fundamentalist churches bought ads in national newspapers announcing: "I'm living proof that Truth can set you free." Above that headline was the photograph of Anne Paulk, self-acknowledged "former lesbian," set free from lesbianism by her belief in Jesus Christ.

The appearance of the ex-gay ads—which a Family Research Council spokesperson called "the Normandy landing in the culture war"—aroused anger within the clerical community, including gay organizations and church groups like the Interfaith Alliance, the United Church of Christ (UCC), the Unitarian Universalist Association (UUA) and a coalition of United Methodist ministers who called the campaign's message "the same old right-wing gay bashing in gentler garb." Clergy, psychologists, and other professionals reminded the media that scientific truth "is not fueling the gay-conversion campaign. Sigmund Freud, behaviorists and others have tried . . . unsuccessfully to develop techniques for changing sexual orientation. Today, most experts reject the notion that people select their sexuality, and indeed many now suspect a genetic link," writes Gayle Holland (LA Weekly, August 12, 1998). "The basic theory of most of these groups is that homosexuality results from a 'broken' relationship with the same-sex parent. Typically, the dynamic involves a cold, distant father and a domineering mother (the bulk of ex-gay literature is about men). Homosexuality is cured by healing the breach. Many ex-gayers are encouraged to bond with an older straight man from their church. They also undergo 'masculinity-building' activities, tossing around the pigskin to stimulate red-blooded hetero drives. Lesbians are urged to trade in their car tools for make-up kits."

Surprisingly, some gay men and lesbians put a positive spin on the ex-gay movement, even while acknowledging the psychological and spiritual damage the ministries are capable of inflicting. Because of the extreme guilt gays and lesbians from fundamentalist faith communities often feel, an ex-gay ministry may be the first place they can freely admit their same-sex attractions. However, ex-gay organizations downplay their role as a social outlet for gays and lesbians. Nor do they admit that the "ex-gay dropout rate is so high; 'ex-ex-gays' now have their own books and Web sites, which describe the movement as a horror show of coercion, guilt and despair," Holland continues. "[In fact], a number of ex-gays report a honeymoon period when forbidden desires subside, followed by a black depression when the feelings come roaring back. Some groups now speak of 'struggling with homosexuality,' rather than of being cured. Many acknowledge that gay fantasies or desires never go away completely, and counsel abstinence or celibacy. In other words, back to the closet."

At Exodus International, the first ex-gay ministry to appear on the national scene in 1976, Benjamin D. Perkins, a divinity school student, paid seventy dollars a week for four years hoping to be transformed from homosexuality to heterosexuality. "Initially, there was a tremendous amount of hope," he told Ariel R. Frank (*Harvard Crimson,* October 27, 1997). "Someone is promising you that the thing that you consider the bane of your existence is going to be eradicated or exorcised." But outside Exodus, as he met more and more gays and lesbians, "the thing I feared most I had to confront," he continued. "I started to realize that gay and lesbian people are just like everyone else."

"The level of suicide within these organizations is astronomical—a fact that makes sense when you take such a large part of yourself and try and hide it or ignore it or actively fight against it," Seth J. Persily told Frank. "Being gay transcends having gay sex. It's a huge part of your identity, and you can never get rid of that."

Kevin Thompson, who once paid an ex-gay ministry to lead him "out of the homosexual lifestyle," called such ministries "fruitless, demeaning, and a waste of time and energy. I can attest that these organizations have no special knowledge, no new thoughts and no novel approaches," he writes as guest columnist in the *St. Paul Pioneer Press* (July 9, 1998). "Their message is the same one thrown at people like me day in and day out. 'You are defective the way you are, and you need to conform to the norm of heterosexuality in order to be acceptable to God, the church and society.'"

Eventually, Kevin escaped those messages of rejection. He acknowledged that God not only loves him as a gay man, but accepts him that way as well. "I owe this freedom, in part, to my experiences with Outpost, [another] 'transforming ministry,'" he writes. "There, I reached the saturation point for negative messages about my supposed defect. At last I turned off the negative religious and societal voices and tuned in to my own heart, where I found complete love, affirmation and peace. I found within me a good man, a compassionate man, a passionate man, a loving man, a creative man, a gay man."

Kevin's realization comes hard for gay men and lesbians everywhere, who must combat "internalized homophobia"—the same negative stereotypes that heterosexuals learn about gay men and lesbians. Except, for them, those lessons often translate into low self-esteem and self-loathing that impede their journey to self-acceptance.

For gay and lesbian ministers, that journey is often even more treacherous.

A Resurrection Experience

Doug Bauder, presently the coordinator of the Gay-Lesbian-Bisexual-Transgendered Student Support Services at Indiana University in Bloomington, served seventeen years as a Moravian minister in Pennsylvania and Wisconsin. Though his current status is "minister without call," Doug feels he could "go back into parish ministry at any time. I may have a hoop or two to jump through, but I could return to the pulpit." In fact, in the absence of a Moravian church in Bloomington, he often preaches and administers sacraments in the local Lutheran church and occasionally serves as hospital chaplain.

"I was brought up in a positive religious atmosphere," Doug recalls. "My particular childhood congregation was very nurturing. The church affirmed me as an individual—with God-given talents worthy of affirmation."

Still, he could not ignore his frequent homosexual fantasies. Although sexually inexperienced during high school, Doug searched the library for information about homosexuality. "But what I was reading didn't connect with what I perceived myself to be," he says. "I thought of homosexuality as an arrested stage of development. I was not sexually active. My masturbatory fantasies were same-sex oriented. But I never defined myself as homosexual. Gay issues in life and on television were more associated with transvestites and leather bars. I assumed I wasn't gay since I didn't identify with those images."

In 1974, while attending seminary, Doug met a woman, already the mother of three children, and fell very much in love with her. "My relationship with Joan—who eventually became my wife—was deep, but at the time, I didn't know who I really was," he continues. "I talked to her about my fears and fantasies. But we were in love with each other. We wanted to make our relationship work. We assumed my same-sex attraction was a passing phase in my adolescence. In seminary, I even tried to redirect my fantasies while I masturbated."

Then, five years into their marriage, "my world was coming apart. I had taken on my second church. I had five children, three of whom I adopted through my wife's first marriage. I was dangerously close to a nervous breakdown. I spent a lot of energy being a superdad and not being true to myself. Still, I had not had any affairs. That which I thought would go away had not, and I felt very trapped. I finally revealed to Joan that what I had always suspected was true. She, too, felt trapped and betrayed. After a year of struggling, we divorced."

Today, Doug and Joan enjoy an amicable relationship, though such was not always the case. "At first, Joan and I weren't talking," Doug explains. "But her fears were eventually assuaged about the kind of gay lifestyle I was going to live. Church authorities knew Joan and I were struggling in our marriage—and they knew why."

To provide an opportunity to work on family issues, the denomination leadership arranged for Doug to take a leave of absence from congregational ministry. "I needed to put my life in perspective," he continues. "The church authorities were hopeful the issue [of homosexuality] would go away. In 1980, the most they could do was recommend counseling. Prior to that, in 1974, at a national provincial synod, the Moravian Church called for a search for wholeness in its response to homosexuals and to homosexuality. The position was not at all condemning, but the thinking was that the church needed to grow in its understanding of sexual orientation."

In 1982, the divorce was finalized. Doug took some time off for counseling—"in essence, to get my life back together. In September of that year, I was offered a parish in Wisconsin—a rural congregation where I pastored for the next ten years."

In the fifth year of that ministry, Doug came out to his congregation. "That experience went exceedingly well," he relates. "Then, I met with the board to request their permission to take a sabbatical. I was determined to write a study guide on sexuality and spirituality. I told them honestly about the project—and how much it meant to me—and they granted the time I needed."

His church never lost members because of Doug's candor. "By the time I came out, I had baptized, married, and buried parishioners," he says. "We had done wonderful things together as a congregation."

But unlike many gay and lesbian clergy, Doug was in a unique position for acceptance because not only had he been married to a woman, he also had several children. "My congregation saw that I was a good father," he explains. "My kids stayed with me for two weekends each month."

Occasionally, Doug's gay friends came to his church to worship, as well. Finally, a parishioner raised a concern with the head of the denomination. "She worried that I might start seeing someone romantically," Doug says. "She said she had no problem with my being romantically involved, but wondered how the community might perceive such a situation. After that, my visibility became more of an issue. I was frequently in touch with eight other Moravian churches. In six of those, I knew of pastoral families who were struggling with their feelings about sons or daughters—or other relatives—who were gay or lesbian. The subject of homosexuality became something of a specialty for me."

Because of Doug's reputation as a resource on sexual orientation issues, he paid a price. Several churches needing a minister passed Doug by as a possibility. Rather than restrict himself to serving the rest of his ministry in one church, he decided to specialize. "I served a year of intense hospital chaplaincy training in 1991 while I was still at the parish," he remembers. "I accomplished that training with the intention of doing a hospice ministry. During that same year, I met the man I'm sharing my life with. He's a tenured professor at the university." The two men struggled with the inconvenience and frustration of long-distance dating for eighteen months. Finally, Marty asked Doug to leave Wisconsin and to move in with him. That Doug had no job in Indiana made no difference to Marty. "I was longing for a relationship. I met Marty, fell in love, and discovered he is also a father—and Jewish. His faith created some interesting points of learning for us both, while his financial position allowed him to provide me a place for a new beginning. Luckily, the university was searching for someone full-time to work with gay and lesbian students."

When their relationship began, Doug was still on-call with the Moravian Church. "But it was clear to me that they perceived me as 'this problem' they had on their hands, because I was involved with Marty," he says. "In my resignation, I clearly stated that I was not moving on to another job, but to a relationship. This was part of God's plan for my life. I was open to the leading of God's spirit."

The head of the denomination asked Doug if he was a "practicing homosexual." "If you're asking whether I express my love to Marty in a sexual way, the answer is yes," Doug told him.

"He commended me for my honesty, but didn't know what to do with that information," Doug continues. "I was on leave of absence for three years with the understanding that I could come back into the ministry. But I had made up my mind. I knew parish ministry would limit my status as a pastor. There are parts of parish pastoring that I miss—like preaching. I love leading worship. But quite frankly, the job at the university gives me a wonderful opportunity to witness to my faith in other ways. I help students to connect to their own sense of who God is. Pastoral support and counseling are gifts I'm still able to use. I've lost some things, and I miss some things. But the work I'm doing now is also a calling."

In retrospect, Doug believes that he became a better person and a better pastor once he affirmed his orientation to his Wisconsin congregation. "While visiting a couple of my parishioners, they told me an incredible story," he says. "Their eldest son had gotten a girl pregnant. The two young people married immediately. No one in their entire family was the wiser. Yet, the parents lived with a lot of shame surrounding those circumstances. They wanted to know if I thought it was wrong for them to love that child as much as they loved their other grandchildren. They said they could never have told another pastor—and couldn't have told me—if I hadn't shared the truth of my life with them. This moment was a real confirmation that in some sense, living in a closet was like living inside a tomb. In that particular church setting, there were many affirmations of my openness. I had a resurrection experience in that congregation—a congregation that deserves a great deal of credit. They lived with their own sense of being second-class citizens because they are rural country folk. And perhaps because of that, they identified with issues of prejudice that were unfounded and unfair."

If two people really love each other, a sexual experience "can be a kind of communion experience," Doug told the couple. "There is no reason to feel shame."

Now, he applies this advice to his own life. "It doesn't happen all the time, but neither do I feel my connection to God every time I participate in a sacrament. I think relating sexually with another person can be very sacramental. At some level, I experienced that with my wife. But there was something lacking in that relationship. I don't think it has to be different for gay and straight people. I have a friend who is severely disabled; he shares many of the details of his life with me. He has a bit of a sexual relationship with one of the other men in the [long-term care facility]. I saw him really loving himself as he talked about how tender Richard was with him. That's a large part of what sexuality is all about—finding someone to enjoy life with."

Should that purpose include same-sex marriage? "I have some trouble with the concept of gay 'marriage' from an ecclesiastical and, perhaps, even a theological point of view," Doug says. "I'm much more comfortable with the concept of services of holy union. Because churches have been blessing everything from pets to little league games, the leap to blessing same-sex relationships shouldn't be that great. Again, part of my thinking is informed by the number of straight weddings I've performed that seem to lack commitment. Having said all of that, I *do* understand the value of gay marriage from a legal perspective. It's still going to be a problem politically, but legally, we who are in committed relationships deserve the same rights as straight couples. Basically, I don't need a wedding cake with two grooms on the top, but I'd welcome the tax breaks, the benefits, and the visitation rights afforded my parents. And I think, because 'marriage' is such a loaded word in our 'weddinged culture,' we'd do well to work on the rights without using the term."

Once Doug established honesty about his sexual orientation—with himself, his community, and his congregation—his patience with fundamentalist views faded. However, he made a startling discovery. "My experience has been that there are many heterosexual Christians 'in the middle' who want to dialog," he says. "For a stranger to tell me what is right or wrong, or that my own struggle or relationship with God is not as valid, or for that stranger to suggest that he or she knows what's right for me—that's unacceptable. I have been invited to a number of congregations who ask about my experiences. When people are willing to dialog about real life issues, progress can be made. Unfortunately, mainline churches have been co-opted by the Radical Right. But we need to go into the churches to say: 'Here's who I am; I need you to know this about me—about us.' The work that I'm about—that all ministers should be about—is to encourage people to be honest."

However, for many clergy serving in conservative churches, the opportunities for honesty remain scarce. Service in repressive fundamentalist traditions requires heterosexual leaders—or, at least, leaders who can play the heterosexual role, called "passing" among gay men and lesbians. These gay and lesbian ministers who have resisted temptation to leave the ministry—or defect to other denominations—witness to their beliefs as clergy in exile.

2

WITNESSING IN EXILE

Walk Like This

Ordained a Baptist minister in a country church more than forty years ago, Glenn Hammett could, at the tender age of six, preach better than the adult ministers in his community. "I was called to go into the ministry," he says. "Yet, because I'm gay, the church rejected my gift. I drifted from job to job for a long time before I found my church home with the International Council of Community Churches (ICCC)."

During his third year in a Baptist-affiliated college, Glenn realized he was gay. "I went to one of my college professors to get counseling for this 'horrible discovery,'" he recalls. "Instead, I got kicked out. That ended my ministry in the Baptist church."

Years later, Glenn returned to college to pursue his calling. Upon graduating, he found "there was no place for the likes of me in the church at that time. Eventually, I was called to a church in Midland, Texas, where I've stayed some fifteen years. The ICCC allows its churches a great deal of autonomy. Most are gay-friendly."

Still, "we're in the Bible Belt here, and people are very conservative," he continues. "Ultra-conservative, right-wing, I would call them."

Glenn observes that countless gays and lesbians have been hurt by churches and by fundamentalist Christians. "One of my parishioners was told by her Baptist pastor never to come back to *his* church again," he explains. "You know, it's a shame we have to have churches like ours. In the mainline denominations, no gay or lesbian ministers that I know around here are open to their congregations. But our church welcomes everyone. Many of our parishioners have never gone to church before in their adult lives. They would never have felt welcome in the churches of their childhoods. And that's a shame."

When he began his ministry, Glenn felt there would never be a place for gay and lesbian ministers in Christian churches. Now, he feels things are changing, but slowly. However, many contemporary churches assume a covertly patronizing stance toward homosexuality. Some churches—like many Episcopal churches following the Lambeth Conference—call congregational meetings during which they recommit themselves to "traditional church views" of human sexuality. Others—like Transforming churches in the United Methodist tradition, or most Southern Baptist churches—acknowledge gay and lesbian members and ministers only when they renounce their sexual orientation or attempt to "repair" it. These churches accept gay and lesbian Christians only when they take steps to become less—or other than—homosexual. The message that true faith cannot embrace dissension is pervasive, damaging, and disruptive.

The experiences of many gay men and lesbians in conservative faith communities suggest that churches smile at pretense but frown at honesty. Their entitlement to both happiness and humanity—found in loving partnerships and candid social interactions—is frequently put at risk. Homosexuality is regarded as a "deep devastation" in need of a fix. That a homosexual's love for a significant other is just as strong, as constructive, as celebratory as a heterosexual's love is discounted and demeaned. "If you're gay, your sexual orientation is suspect," writes reporter Justin Chinn.[1] "There are certainly plenty of heterosexuals who lead unfulfilling lives, . . . but no one blames their misery on their sexual orientation."

Yet, duplicity often results when a church unknowingly selects a gay or lesbian minister to fill its pulpit. Because most Christian professions of faith designate homosexual *acts* as stumbling blocks to salvation, gay and lesbian clergy, even if accepted by a particular church or denomination, are expected, if they cannot change, to lead lives of celibacy. Sometimes, once their orientation is disclosed, they are even driven from the pulpit. Whatever their machinations for "dealing" with gay and lesbian ministers, these churches demand that their witnesses to God's love deliver their message as expatriates to the integrity they have woven into their lives.

In 1981, a former male lover of Rembert Truluck, then a religion professor at Baptist College at Charleston (now Charleston Southern University) and an ordained Southern Baptist minister, told the college's Board of Trustees of their romantic relationship. The outing was not vicious, vengeful, or vindictive; according to Rembert's "friend," he had merely followed God's command. "The college trustees called a secret meeting," Rembert relates. "No written record was kept of it. Even the college president was not called to the meeting; he was informed by telephone to secure my resignation without delay."

Rembert told the president, a heterosexual friend aware of Rembert's orientation, that he would resign "if my resignation would be of any help to you." The president said that the trustees had requested the resignation, and it was out of his hands. Rembert tried to find work after leaving the college, but for a while he couldn't. "A minister in a church is conditioned to be dependent on the church for his existence," Rembert explains. "When something like this happens—and despite the years I spent in the pulpit, I couldn't go back to parish pastoring—you have none of that security. You're in a jungle without any preparation."

Months later, Rembert asked a colleague at Baptist College if anyone ever mentioned him. "It's as though you were never here," he said, "and as though the resignation had never happened. You just—disappeared."

Rembert grew up in Clinton, South Carolina, a small town where many citizens earned their livelihoods in the employ of textile plants. The presence of Presbyterian College contributed to a more liberal social climate for the town. "At about the time I entered public school, I began to realize that I was attracted to other boys, but not to girls," Rembert explains. "This awareness grew stronger into high school and until I was eighteen years old. Of course, I dated girls. I even pretended to be interested in them. However, I kept my homosexuality to myself—except for the occasional sexual experiences I had with other boys."

During the summer of 1952, following his high school graduation, Rembert experienced God's call to ministry, entered college, and even served as pastor of a Southern Baptist church while attending Furman University in Greenville, South Carolina. By 1968, he had earned a doctorate degree in sacred theology. "Serving as a student pastor of several churches in both Kentucky and South Carolina during my seminary days, I learned about the destructive power of sick religion as well as the great power and love of Christ to change people into God's children," he says.

In 1959, Rembert married and began to build a home and family, "just as I was expected to do as a Southern Baptist minister," he continues. "My wife and I had three beautiful children. Everything seemed 'normal' to everyone on the outside looking in. But I was gay and frustrated and in secret pain that I could not discuss with anyone. I went to three different psychiatrists for help"—all of whom told him that psychiatry could not change sexual orientation. "One thing that strikes me lately is the large number of gay people who have been married and have children," he says. "My circumstances are not that unusual."

Now, Rembert lives in Oakland, California. Through his Internet presence, called "Steps to Recovery from Bible Abuse," his books (including one based on research and personal insights for his Web site), and his workshops, he strives to be an effective presence in the "social and spiritual war zone" created by organized Christianity. "Low self-esteem among lesbian and gay Christians was the main issue motivating my published Bible studies from the beginning," Rembert confides. "I developed later studies to deal with many other pressures, problems, and issues faced by homosexuals in an environment of homophobic hate, religious oppression, abusive use of the Bible against gays and lesbians, and the persistent problem of homophobia within the gay and lesbian community. We live in the midst of church and community alienation, and suffer from chronic internalized and horizontal homophobia."

Now, though Rembert's denomination has exiled him, he continues to have a strong faith "in God and in Jesus Christ as the best way to tell us what to do with our lives. Jesus told us to keep our worship simple and people-centered, and that's the way we should do it. Instead, our churches—and even the MCC is guilty of this—seat people in rows. From that perspective, we look at the backs of people's heads. Jesus' methods are obvious when you read the Gospels. Everything was new. That he included everybody in his teachings was also unheard of in an era of exclusivity. When Jesus fed the five thousand, he gathered people from many different backgrounds together to eat. That was certainly new. The experience of the new and the revolutionary in one's life is the very essence, the very spirit, of Jesus Christ. Christians need to be open to that. Unfortunately, the church continues to live in the sixteenth century. The Reformation began and ended with Martin Luther."

The sentiment currently found in many churches, Rembert says, is certainly to follow Jesus' teachings, but only up to a point. "As Christians, we no longer want to pay the price of belief," he explains. "Jesus always meant for us to pattern our lives on the basis of helping someone else. When doing something on another's behalf is our guiding principle, truth comes from directions we really can't control."

In Rembert's opinion, Southern Baptist churches will not accept openly gay and lesbian leadership for another generation or two. "Paige Patterson, president of the Southern Baptist Convention, is a real homophobic legalist. He is the epitome of the hypocrisy found in the church." Patterson, elected president of the Southern Baptist Convention during an annual conference in Salt Lake City on June 9, 1997, is generally regarded as one of the architects of the conservative resurgence in the Southern Baptist Convention that began in 1979. He spearheaded the campaign in Salt Lake City to codify the tenets that wives should graciously submit to their husbands, and the church and state should recognize a family defined only by procreating male and female spouses. "I know of a pastor of a prominent Southern Baptist church who is gay and closeted. He and I have become friends through my current ministry. Yet Patterson denies that Southern Baptist congregations even have gays and lesbians in them—much less that a gay man would be called to the ministry of a Southern Baptist church." (The Southern Baptist Convention prohibits the ordination of women to the ministry.)

Despite Rembert's terse criticism of the Southern Baptist tradition, he insists that he is not against the church,"but I'm definitely against the abuses of the church. We're going through tumultuous and exciting times. I don't know whether the church will turn around or not. It will take some action on the part of God, that's for sure. After all, churches have an incredible amount of power."

Churches are plagued by two serious problems—problems that will not be easily resolved. "All denominations are self-destructive and in denial of what Jesus taught," Rembert says. "We have a tremendous need for a one-on-one type of ministry. But the church has been configured into something other than what we see in Jesus' ministry. Automatically, churches become engaged with their members in a struggle for power. To win that struggle, the church has to brainwash its parishioners. Therefore, the first problem revolves around the way clergy persist in doing church. The second problem is that most people—particularly gay and lesbian people—have had experiences with oppressive and abusive authority figures. Whether you hate your father because of his abuse of power, or you've been fired by your boss, or any door is shut in your face because of your sexual orientation—well, when a pastor positions himself as someone with ultimate power over you, a problem evolves quickly. When I served as pastor in both Baptist and MCC churches, I was under attack all the time by people who harbored unresolved anger toward parents and other authority figures. There has to be a better way than the way we're doing church now."

A place to start might be a reexamination of the relationship ministers have with their parishioners. "Jesus *listened* before he told his followers what to do," Rembert explains. "Even modern doctors listen to their patients before initiating treatment. But ministers think the same slogans and treatments work for everybody. What results from such a standardized approach is an overwhelming use of the Bible as a weapon. What's more, church leadership is sometimes pretty sick, and they're the ones wielding that Bible. What's happening now reminds me of a quote by Adolph Hitler. He said it's easier to get people to believe a big lie rather than a small lie. Many religious leaders tell big lies about our lives, just like Hitler told big lies about various groups. Hitler was insane; he plunged the world into horror. But what's the difference between him and the pastor who brainwashes parishioners so they don't like each other? Or they don't trust one another? Or they hate each other? All it takes is a powerful, strong personality that can manipulate people. And that's what's happening to many Christians over issues of homosexuality."

How can faith communities find their way back to reconciliation? "First of all, churches need to stop saying that the scriptures mean only what church hierarchy says they mean," he says. "They must be willing to admit that neither Jesus nor the Bible condemned homosexuals. After all, the legalism of the prevailing religious leaders—the protectors of the status quo—killed Jesus. Legalism will also kill us—unless we resist. The only cure for legalism is the new life and freedom that come into our lives when we invite Jesus to take control. When I taught religion courses at Baptist College, my main concern was to teach students to see the Bible for the first time. Yet those students came into my classes with all kinds of preconceptions and misconceptions. They had already been told what the Bible meant. They felt they didn't need to take a new look. Although I never specifically spoke in favor of homosexuality in my college classes, I never condemned gays and lesbians, either. But some of my students complained to the college president that I didn't spend any class time criticizing homosexuals. Now that increasing numbers of gays and lesbians say we are deserving of respect, the church has decided to come after us with sick religion."

Rembert defines "sick religion" as one whose purpose is "to hurt people. An underlying characteristic is an arrogant, absolute certainty about everything. Sick religious leaders, churches, and denominations often pose as experts in every field of study—and that includes science, religion, psychology, politics, and sociology. They claim that anyone who disagrees with their views is evil. They demean and belittle people, and make them feel shame and guilt if they do not comply with religion as seen by the dominant group, to which they demand absolute allegiance."

Because of the influences of sick religion, Rembert says, religious wars are developing. Through his ministry, he urges gay and lesbian Christians to fight their fear of the conflicts that will ultimately result—that are resulting now. "Fear makes people vulnerable," he says. "I know of one Southern Baptist church where a new pastor preached a strong sermon attacking homosexuals. Following the sermon, several church leaders approached the pastor to tell him that the sermon hurt a lot of leaders in the church who had gay and lesbian children whom they loved and accepted. The pastor never mentioned homosexuals in his sermons again. He remained as pastor of that church for twenty-five years. I know this story is true, because two of those church leaders were my parents, and the pastor became my friend."

Rembert praises religious leaders who have taken steps to stop the invective from their pulpits against gays and lesbians in the name of Christianity. "Still, traditional churches may be of little help to gay and lesbian Christians in building a strong spiritual life that will sustain them throughout the religious wars. No one should be afraid to reach out to new and unfamiliar resources and to take 'the road less traveled' to find freedom from fear and spiritual oppression and abuse." Even Jesus challenged traditional beliefs and practices of his day. "Jesus revealed to his parents that he was different and that he had a special mission in life that they did not understand," Rembert says. "When his parents found Jesus in the Temple, they were surprised and said exactly what a lot of parents say to gay and lesbian children when they come out: 'How could you do this to us!' Jesus did not apologize to his parents for 'coming out' and acting on who he really was. He simply said that he had to be true to himself and left it at that. His mother was loving and accepting even when she did not understand. We need more mothers like that!"

Perhaps, Rembert says, we need more churches like that, too. "When are we going to stop beating our heads bloody against the brick wall of homophobic churches, trying to gain acceptance into religious traditions and institutions that have lost their own spiritual credibility and relevance to today's world?" he asks. "Churches are living in the Dark Ages. They cling to attitudes and practices that the rest of our society outgrew centuries ago. Only at church are people expected to check their brains at the door and let someone else do their thinking for them."

Rembert jars the thinking of church leaderships standing against gay and lesbian inclusion by reminding parishioners to examine closely the uses of their hard-earned money in the name of Christ. "What has the church done with its great wealth?" he asks. "Recently, the Mormon Church gave over a million dollars to fight against the recognition of gay and lesbian loving, committed relationships in both Alaska and Hawaii. James Kennedy and other leaders of the great spiritual ignorance movement raised, then spent, a fortune to advertise the misguided toxic religion of the ex-gay movement. The churches could, however, solve the needs of the poor and homeless to demonstrate their sincerity in following Jesus, who said, 'Inasmuch as you have done it to one of the least of these my brothers and sisters, you have done it to me.' Søren Kierkegaard asked over 150 years ago: Is it really the same thing when Jesus said, 'Sell what you have and give it to the poor,' as when the priest says, 'Sell what you have and give it to me'? We would have a solution to the plight of the homeless in every city in America if the churches would open their doors to the homeless and provide them places to sleep in the unused space that every church has every night of the week in every city."

Instead, some churches designate significant funds to fuel the ex-gay movement—claiming, with little statistical data to support them, that prayer and diligence can lead gays and lesbians away from their "lifestyle" to a heterosexual or celibate life in Jesus. In November 1998, Thom Cooper, a high school friend, contacted Rembert via electronic mail to apprise him of his prior attempts to turn away from his homosexuality through an ex-gay ministry. "Frustrated at my inability to control my mind, at some point I addressed God and told Him that I was accepting myself just as He had created me—as a gay man," Thom wrote. "I was not going to continue fighting His creativity, as I had come to believe I was acceptable in His eyes. At that point, I began a new life by accepting myself as a gay man. That acceptance has brought me great happiness and a new self-image that is positive, despite rejection by my dad and stepmother, and my only brother."

Such a mindset, Rembert says, is faithful to "Jesus' positive encouragement to live and tell your truth. In Matthew 5:16, Jesus said, . . . 'let your light shine before others, so that they may see your good works and give glory to your Father in heaven.' Coming out is part of your witness for Christ as a gay or lesbian believer."

However, when gay and lesbian Christians come out to friends, family, or fellow believers, they must exercise caution and common sense. Rembert tells of a sixteen-year-old boy named Allen who asked his father for advice about how to handle being gay. "Put a gun in your mouth and pull the trigger," his father replied curtly.

Although some gays and lesbians may find parental love to be elusive or conditional, the bottom line of Jesus' ministry is crystal clear. "Love and acceptance for wounded and rejected people is not just a major theme of the

Bible," Rembert says. "It is the reason the Bible was written in the first place. God's love is a 'free gift,' which is the meaning of grace—an unmerited favor, or an unearned gift. To live a lie, as Allen's father would have preferred of his son, is to live outside the will of God. Lying to yourself and to others about who you really are is spiritual self-sabotage. To all those so-called Christians who would be so arrogant as to assert that they *know* God's feelings about homosexuality, I would say this: God is not discovered at the end of an argument. The name of God is constantly emerging with fresh meaning."

However, their philosophies closely parallel the beliefs and prejudices of various faith communities. To the degree that they are able to push their agenda, they can influence the stand on ordination and acceptance issues of a variety of churches. The Ramsey Colloquium, for example, cloaked anti-gay stereotypes and generalizations—like the incapacity of gay men and lesbians to sustain long-term relationships—in the language of academia. If the ex-gay movement grows or fundamentalist views continue to infiltrate mainline denominations, gay and lesbian ministers will certainly find ministries of integrity and inclusion increasingly difficult to establish. Ultimately, gay and lesbian clergy within certain denominations may be forced to choose between maintaining silence within the closet's restraints or risking the consequences of honesty and affirmation. For these ministers, the risks of asserting one's beliefs are considerable.

The Things That Make For Peace

That the reconciliation of homosexuality and Christianity must lead to change in either a homosexual's behavior or orientation is a widely-supported position within various church traditions. Some churches tacitly accept gay and lesbian ministers who do not act on their sexual drives. Other faith communities become quite shrill in their condemnation of ministers whose homosexual orientation they've just discovered, leaving it impossible for the newly out clergy to witness to God's grace and mercy. In fact, cadres of believers live close to the fundamentalist stream of consciousness—hating the sin, yet scarcely understanding why it's wrong to hate the sinner, too. Conservative Christians have finally come out of *their* closets and "want to speak their native language. To hell with it," says James Neuchterlein, editor of the conservative magazine *First Things,* of criticism that ex-gay ministries merely disguise prejudices. "This is what we believe. Accept it or not."

Acceptance could, on the conditions of celibacy or transformation, which many gay and lesbian ministers find personally unacceptable, produce harmony within Christian faith communities. They would receive not only God's forgiveness but also the forgiveness of their congregations. But many gay and lesbian ministers lead spiritually resonant lives in monogamous, committed relationships with their partners—or, they hope to establish such relationships in the future. However, for both mainline and fundamentalist denominations, a same-sex relationship, no matter how closely it resembles a heterosexual marriage, seldom warrants affirmation, respect, or blessing.

Though most denominations would prefer to sweep issues of same-sex relationships under the carpet, the topic keeps arising. The Southern Baptist Convention, the nation's largest Protestant denomination, declared God's intended role for males to be that of provider and protector, while the divinely-ordained feminine role remains to nurture and assist. In a time of "growing crisis in the family," wives must learn once more to submit to their husbands—a tenet "clearly revealed in Scripture," says R. Albert Mohler, Jr., president of the Southern Baptist Theological Seminary in Louisville, Kentucky. "It is God's pattern."

Catholicism teaches that all sexual ethics rest on the principle that every genital act must be open to the possibility of conception within the structure of heterosexual marriage.[2] Therefore, all nontraditional families violate God's pattern, according to Pope John Paul II, who made his statement shortly after Italian newspapers covered a United States court decision opening the way for unmarried couples, including gay and lesbian couples, to adopt children. For the Vatican, like most conservative churches, including the Southern Baptist Convention, the only acceptable "lifestyle" for the "incurable homosexual" is mandatory, lifetime celibacy. "The Vatican's insistence on imposing the medieval discipline of celibacy as a way of life on all homosexual people today rankles faithful gay Catholics like me," writes Chuck Colbert, co-chair of the Gay and Lesbian Alumni of the University of Notre Dame and Saint Mary's College.[3] "From my perspective, celibacy, not freely chosen, is repressed sexuality, utterly irreconcilable with a gay person's identity, self-respect, and dignity. In other words, obligatory celibacy is tantamount to not experiencing a fully human life."

But the conviction that only heterosexual sex makes sense—that is, because only heterosexual intercourse is capable of producing a child, God intends genital activity to be preserved for opposite-sex partners—underlies the teachings of the Roman Catholic Church, according to John M. Haas, president of the Pope John Center for the Study of Ethics in Health Care.[4] "The church's teaching on sexuality is really no more difficult to understand than understanding that men and women were made for one another, for love, for bonding, for engendering children and establishing a family," he explains. "We Catholics know that if people do not use their bodies according to nature's design, they may suffer. This is true if people overeat, do not get enough rest, drink too much, use drugs. This is certainly the case with homosexual practices. . . . All [the church's] teachings are but different ways of expressing her concern for human happiness."

Father Jim Morris also attempts to find happiness through a spirituality largely defined by the Roman Catholic Church. Ordained in 1989, Jim was stationed in Our Lady of Lourdes in Queens Village, New York City, for six years. Jim began a leave of absence from his parish when he fell in love with another man—despite the fact that his congregation already knew of his homosexual orientation. "I don't know that I did anything consciously to lead anyone to think one way or the other until 1994," he explains. "That was five years into my ministry. It was something that was not exactly planned."

In January 1994, Jim, along with hundreds of other gay men and lesbians, signed a petition to sponsor a state antidiscrimination bill that would include sexual orientation. "The petition was printed in a full-page ad in the *New York Times*," he says. "I didn't think twice about signing it. It was the right and just thing to do. A few months later, the ad appeared. It identified the signers as gay and lesbian people."

"Who are we?" the ad stated. "We are your relatives, your co-workers, and your neighbors who happen to be lesbians and gay men. We live and pay taxes in New York, where state laws don't stop people from discriminating against us in employment, housing, education, credit, and public accommodations."

Shortly after the ad's appearance, a columnist from *Newsday* magazine called. "For some unknown reason, he pulled my name out of the list and called our chancery office to find out if I was a priest in good standing," Jim continues. "A public relations officer told him that while I was in good standing, I was a 'troublemaker.'"

Why a troublemaker? "A year before, the bishop of our diocese had published a pastoral letter that reiterated the Vatican's statement that homosexuality is an intrinsic moral disorder," he explains. "I criticized him for repeating a destructive theological stance."

Bill Reel's *Newsday* column appeared on Father's Day 1994. "I wrote a letter to my bishop and told him the column would appear," Jim continues. "I contemplated buying every copy of *Newsday* in a four-square-mile radius of my parish—a parish of about twelve thousand Catholics, three thousand of whom attended our church."

Aware of the Pope's pronouncements about homosexuality, Jim worried about the potential aftermath of his congregation's discovery of his orientation. "Surprisingly, I received scores of supportive letters and telephone calls from parishioners who thanked me for coming out," Jim says. "They told me how much it meant to them. Then, one really poignant thing happened. Our parish was in the middle of a major development drive to raise six hundred thousand dollars for various essential repairs. We had hired a firm to raise the funds for us. When the president of the fund-raising firm discovered that I had been outed in *Newsday*, he tried to breach the contract. He was afraid his company couldn't raise the required funds because of the 'scandal.'"

However, the church received only one negative telephone call. A parishioner threatened to withdraw his pledge of one thousand dollars because of

Jim's disclosure. By the end of his conversation with the head pastor, the man changed his mind.

"Strangely enough, my bishop never addressed the issue with me," Jim continues. "However, in that same month—June 1994—just after the Pope proclaimed that the question of women's ordination was closed and could no longer be discussed, he suspended me from all parochial duties. This happened shortly after I addressed the Vatican's sexist stance in a homily, which a visiting priest heard. Apparently, this particular priest didn't like the reference and complained directly to the bishop."

Only once during the meetings leading to Jim's suspension did the bishop allude to his coming out. "I think that was a terrible thing you did—coming out as a gay priest," the bishop whispered harshly, as Jim stood at the open office door.

"I think it was the most important thing I've ever done," Jim replied before he left.

Jim, the parish staff, and the head pastor tried to determine how the church might deal with the bishop's "irrational decision." Ultimately, they decided simply to ignore the suspension. "The bottom line is that I continued in my ministry," Jim says. "In October, the bishop told our vicar that he knew I was functioning as a priest. He could have removed the vicar from his position because of his complicity, but chose not to. I don't know why."

In September 1995, Jim requested a personal leave of absence. "I made this request of my own free will," he explains. "The bishop had nothing to do with it. You see, I had fallen in love. I could no longer lead the celibate life of a parish priest."

Jim still considers himself a priest in active ministry. "I continue to be a social worker. I view my work as ministerial and as part of a wider plan. My work is God's design. I also continue to serve ministerially in the Catholic church. I preside at liturgies of Dignity [an organization of gay and lesbian Catholics, their families, friends, and loved ones designed to promote reform in the Roman Catholic Church] in New York as local chaplain. Also, on occasion, I am called by friends and acquaintances to preside at liturgies, to baptize their children and to bury their dead, all without the bishop's knowledge."

While serving Our Lady of Lourdes, Jim often experienced a profound sense of loneliness. "Priests are in such a privileged position—playing an essential role in important moments in people's lives and their loving commitments made to one another in marriage and being at their sick beds—and their death beds. When all is said and done, everyone goes home and leaves me, their priest, in an empty church."

When Dignity became part of Jim's life, he still could not escape the loneliness. "After those meetings, I would return to my parish community, knowing I would not be among the gay community for another week or more," he explains. "Even though I knew I was a gay man since I was a teenager and had been in a relationship for years before I even considered the ordained ministry, the one thing that had never occurred to me was that, down deep inside, I had a need for a community that understood me for what and who I was. That's the definition of a worshiping community. Although I was part of a parish community, there was still a need within me for a community of peers who were just like me—who were gay—who could come together and see God somewhat differently. The need for a worshiping community, articulated by the Second Vatican Council, was never so clear as when I came out. Coming out enabled me to worship God more effectively and more fully, though it inevitably meant the loss of my parish congregation."

Although the demands of the Roman Catholic Church and the prejudice of superiors ultimately drove him away, Jim never took his calling lightly. "As I look back on it, my father's death, combined with my turning thirty a year later, impacted my decision to enter the priesthood," he explains. "At that point in my life, I was reexamining where I was, where I was headed in terms of the meaning of life, and what I wanted to do with the rest of my life. At thirty, a life in the ministry occurred to me. I began to explore the possibilities by participating in the Brooklyn Diocese's Contact Program, which was designed for men and women considering the possibility of ministry but were not quite ready to make a full commitment. I participated for three years before finally making the decision to enter seminary. I was out at the time—to myself and to a few friends. In fact, I had been partnered until I was twenty-seven. At that time, although I knew I might have to fight sexual desire occasionally, I was willing to lead a celibate lifestyle. I gave a lot of prayerful consideration to that vow. Part of the reason for my three-year delay before entering seminary related to a fear I entertained during that period. What if I met someone in seminary to whom I was attracted? How would that affect my decision?"

His relationship with Jeff, Jim feels, coincides with God's wishes for his life. The church provides a model for that relationship and brings peace to the life Jim and his partner have found in each other. However, the Roman Catholic Church does not honor what they have. "God's intent for human sexuality is to help human beings have deeper relationships with one another," he explains. "God wants for us to have relationships so deep that they mirror the very life of God, which is itself a relationship—the ultimate relationship—the relationship that is the Trinity."

Running From Who We Are

Fundamentalist churches—particularly Southern Baptist, Church of God, Assemblies of God, and Pentecostal faith communities—create a sense of camaraderie among parishioners that rivals most mainline churches. Often, their services are informal and celebratory. Because of the perceived love and support from charismatic Christians (no matter how conditional), gay and lesbian ministers in these traditions sometimes have an even tougher time with self-acceptance than do clergy in mainline denominations. They question whether the sense of human bonding after coming out, even to themselves, will ever match the kind of affection they feel from their parishioners. Consequently, fundamentalist clergy are driven deeper into the closet, where they seriously question their spiritual integrity and value. For them, coming out often means relinquishing a calling to which they have devoted much of their lives.

Chad Tilley's parents raised him in the United Methodist Church, but a mainline denominational background didn't stop him from joining a cult—at least, that's the way his parents saw it. "In college, I got hooked up with a fundamentalist church," he explains. "Looking back, my reaction is an incredulous one. At first, Mom and Dad wanted to withdraw me from college. Subconsciously, I ran so far to the right because—well, I was essentially running from myself."

Chad's first acknowledgment of his homosexuality tore him apart. "I've had to work hard to reconcile, as much as possible, what I believe with what I am," he explains. "One man in our church—a straight man—let me cry on his shoulder. He felt it was okay to be gay, but it's not okay to act on that. I went thirty-six years without doing anything. I was a card-carrying member of True Love Waits [an organization committed to teaching young adults to save sex until marriage]. However, my choice now is not to fight anymore. I'm gay. I have to accept that fact."

Although Chad has accepted his orientation, he can't say yet "that homosexuality is not morally inferior to heterosexuality. I know what I'd like to say; I'd like to say, 'No; there's no difference.' But calling sin sin is really hard." He pauses. "I used to be black and white about sin. Now I see more in shades of gray. For me, it's not a cop-out. I see all kinds of things as sin; sin separates me from God. But other things separate me from God, too. If I eat too much at the church buffet or if I sleep with someone outside marriage, I am sinning. If I'm a greedy person, then, to me, it's a sin not to help the poor. Selectively acknowledging my orientation has made me a more compassionate person, sure. But it also allows me to see how easy it is to be fallen. For my salvation, I'm trusting in the sheer grace of God. If it's not my homosexuality that keeps me out of heaven, then it'll be something else."

Seven years ago, Chad's youngest brother—his middle brother is heterosexual, but "has good taste in draperies"—came out to their family. "However, he didn't take a dramatic turn toward fundamentalism the way I did," he says. "When he came out, I realized that I wasn't admitting something honest about myself. I prayed for him not to have to put up with all the things I did, like the temptation and the guilt. He said it was easier for him to come out than for me because the world's views had changed. I began to adjust, though. I did more research to see what I really believe. I remember going to a friend's house and confiding in him that my brother was gay. It was tearing me apart! I *know* how fundamentalists feel when they find out someone's gay. Their feelings *are* genuine. Before I came out to myself, I towed the line and talked the talk. I believed in the philosophy of 'love the sinner but hate the sin.' That's hard to do. Lots of people say it, but few can pull it off. Many hide behind the rhetoric, and what they say really comes from hate."

For several years, Chad, now thirty-seven, served as a youth pastor in a nondenominational fundamentalist church. Although he is not actively ministering now, he is still drawn to the ministry, "but maybe with a church less charismatic than what I've been accustomed to."

During his ministry, Chad ran into an old friend at the North Carolina Gay Film Festival. Previously, the possibility that his friend might be gay never crossed his mind.

"I guess we don't have to ask each other *that question*," Chad commented wryly.

The other man laughed. "Let's get together for lunch someday soon," he replied. "Not tomorrow, though. I've got some church business to take care of."

"As it turns out," Chad explains, "he's a minister with the local Metropolitan Community Church. Knowing him, and knowing he's gay, helped me out a lot. I feel more hopeful about my own self-acceptance."

As a minister in the early stages of coming out, Chad isn't quite sure what God intends for human sexuality. "Procreation is one important purpose, of course, but the earth has been populated for a long, long time," he says. "God's intent is also for pleasure and for communion and intimacy far beyond sex. In the Song of Solomon, there is incredible passion and enjoyment and communion going on there. Homosexuality, though. I just don't know. I would *like* to think it is part of God's design. Maybe it's not a sin. But if it *is* a sin, it's no greater a sin than any other. And I'm not completely convinced it *is* a sin."

What about those biblical passages often used to condemn homosexuality? "I lean toward wishful thinking," Chad replies, "and the idea that homosexuality is not what those passages are talking about. There are other restrictions, like men having sex with women during their period. The Pauline stuff is harder to deal with. Paul is, of course, not without his critics. He's a man, after all, no matter how close he was to God. He's subject to making mistakes just as much as anybody else."

In Chad's view, a gay minister would probably be accepted into his former church community, provided he remained celibate and fought hard against his orientation. "I know of a church pastor—in a tradition similar to mine—who is an ex-gay," Chad relates. "This guy has tried really hard. He's married and has kids. But he's not without temptation and without thought. There's yet another man who struggles daily with homosexual temptation.

He's counseled me to live as he does, but he is such an unhappy person. Because he is so bitter, he isn't much fun to be around." He clears his throat. "I crave the intimacy and communion of a committed relationship with another man," he confides. "Always, in my life, I have enjoyed relationships with men—on the friendship level, you understand. We'd spend time together. Laugh. Joke. Then, they went home to their wives. It would have been great if one of them had been going home with me."

Chad admires the writings of Tony Campolo, a liberal Baptist minister and professor of sociology at Eastern College in St. Davids, Pennsylvania, and president of the Evangelical Association for the Promotion of Education. To be a Christian, Campolo feels, a homosexual must remain celibate. (His wife, Peggy, doesn't share his sentiment, a point they make during their speaking engagements on college campuses. In God's eyes, she believes, the love between two same-sex partners is as highly valued as the love between two heterosexuals.)[5]

Occasionally, Chad grapples with Campolo's philosophy of male chastity. Campolo feels that two men can live together in love, but to remain in God's grace, they can never experience sexual intimacy. "But how far can you go without the physical relationship being classified as sexual?" Chad asks in a frustrated voice. "I could live without sodomy. But could I live without French kissing? I don't know. Campolo agrees that gay people are born that way. He advocates that we should have relationships and express ourselves physically, but no more physically than petting. In some ways, I admire that structure. I wonder if that's where I'll ultimately end up. I don't know. I wouldn't want to be in a relationship where my partner and I didn't touch at all." He pauses. Finally, he confesses a deep longing. "I want reconciliation in my heart and mind so that I can see homosexual expression as a sacred act."

Faith and Being Gay Matter

Although her denomination, the Christian Church (Disciples of Christ), is nationally on record as opposing the ordination of gays and lesbians, Christine Leslie was openly ordained in May 1981 by the denomination's Northern California/Nevada Region. "Our denomination runs the gamut," Chris explains. "It depends on the congregation and the setting. I would describe the denomination as predominately moderate, with our more liberal regions on the east and west coasts. The conservative and fundamentalist folks are mostly in the south, midwest, and western areas of the country. I was fortunate to have gone to seminary in a liberal region."

However, she didn't stay there. "And had I not learned about Jim Fowler's 'stages of faith,' I don't think I would have been able to stay in the church or ordained ministry these eighteen years," she says. "When I learned about the 'stages of faith,' I came to understand why we humans have so many ways of believing what we believe. There is a stage of literalism, or 'fundamentalism,' through which we need to go in order to learn the fundamentals of the faith we are being taught. Without them, we have no foundation on which to build a faith that can grow and mature. When we don't grow past the fundamentalist, or 'literalist,' stage, we remain spiritual children dependent on external religious authorities and their beliefs. Many people do this for many reasons, and simply never make the spiritual maturation journey from secondhand religion to firsthand faith."

Though raised in the South, Chris grew up amid the liberal aspects of her denomination; she didn't know fundamentalism existed. Having studied the "stages of faith" and having watched her sister's twenty-year involvement with fundamentalism, she learned why fundamentalism could be so appealing. "My sister was a Christian fundamentalist until she realized she could be her own person," Chris explains. "As she allowed herself to become less dependent on an external source of spiritual authority, she became more accepting of her own lesbianism from which she had been running since her teens. She almost committed suicide because of the homophobic abuse she received at the hands of fundamentalist leaders of the church she was in. I thank God for the inner spiritual and emotional strength she had built inside herself during those years that finally made it possible for her to break free."

Chris believes that fundamentalists experience a childlike dependency on an external system of rules and regulations "that minimize what they have to think and decide for themselves. For them, God is an external authority, not an internal reality. The scriptures are to be taken literally rather than carefully. Believers are going to heaven; nonbelievers are going to hell. People must abide by rigid and narrow definitions of what it is to be human and how they are to relate." Such a paradigm works as long as a person has no conflict between "who they are and what they are told to be," Chris continues. "When conflict does emerge, the journey from secondhand religion to firsthand faith can begin. It's the journey my sister made, and it's the one that many gay and lesbian people take as they come to terms with their God-given sexual orientation."

Through prayer, study, meditation, and communal worship, firsthand faith involves experiencing a direct and trusting personal relationship with the Sacred One. "Because God is internal and eternal—not external—firsthand faith is a person's ultimate reliance on an internal sense of God's presence and love that may or may not be nurtured by an external religious system. I believe this is what Jesus came to teach and show us. It's why I can—and do—remain in the ministry to this day."

During her eighteen-year ministry, Chris has served in a number of capacities, including hospital and hospice chaplaincy, and drug and alcohol counseling. She also cofounded and served as executive director of the Habitat for Humanity affiliate in Newark, New Jersey. Reflecting back on her journey, including parish ministry, Chris tells of returning to the closet in 1984. "I accepted the Glen Ridge Congregation Church's call to be their associate minister," she explains. "I nearly lost my sanity because of the duplicity with which I had to live. It was a very rough way to relearn that no job is worth the hell of hiding when ministry is all about being a person of integrity and honesty. I have not hidden my sexual orientation from my employers since."

Currently, Chris and her partner, Martha Dyson, an Episcopal priest, live in Williston, Vermont, where they moved in 1997 so Martha could serve as the associate priest at St. Paul's Episcopal Cathedral in Burlington. Several months after the move, Chris founded Triangle Ministries—a Center for Lesbian and Gay Spiritual Development—where she provides pastoral counseling and spiritual direction primarily to gays and lesbians who want help integrating their sexual identity with their spiritual journey.

In a way, Chris was destined for ordained ministry. "My dad is a Disciples of Christ minister," she explains. "Because of his liberated understanding of Christianity, I grew up in a fairly healthy faith system. As a child, I was introduced to a loving and nonjudgmental God. I was spared the horrors of some folks. After graduating from high school, I went off to college to study voice and opera at the Conservatory of Music at the University of Cincinnati. Like most kids when they leave home and go to college, I had quit going to church. At the end of my junior year, having become an accomplished guitarist, I was invited to lead folk masses in a local Roman Catholic congregation. Little did I know at the time that God was also inviting me to reexamine the direction of my life. Leading music for worship for two years spurred me to question my decision to pursue opera as a career. By the spring of 1975, I was finally beginning to realize that God had not called me to be an opera diva."

During a camping trip that same spring, Chris experienced a personal call to ministry. "It was a Sunday morning and I was sitting on the side of a mountain," she says. "The air was very still. It was very quiet, very calm. I thought, 'I need some concrete direction here.' I had a Bible with me. After opening it, the pages literally blew open to the twenty-third chapter of John, where I read: 'Peter? Do you love me?' Jesus asked. 'Yes, I love you.' Then, Jesus replied, 'Then feed my sheep.' I finally knew what God wanted me to do. I just didn't know how this calling would work itself out."

In short order, Chris decided to withdraw from the Masters in Opera program. She went from teaching voice lessons and giving recitals to delivering medications all over a hospital eight times a day as a pharmacy messenger. One spring day in 1976, during a stop in the Intensive Care Unit, Chris saw a young woman on her knees beside an older woman who lay in the hospital bed.

"What's going on?" Chris whispered to the head nurse.

The nurse explained that after the patient's routine hysterectomy, she had thrown a blood clot and was now "brain dead." Her daughter had arrived to say good-bye before life support was removed.

Chris asked the nurse if she would be sending for the hospital chaplain. "I wouldn't call that bozo for all the money in the world," she replied. "He is such a jerk; he only makes things worse for people."

Chris was stunned by her candor. Even more, she was saddened for the young woman who wept alone at her mother's side.

Then, as Chris turned to leave the room, a golden figure appeared in the doorway. She felt enveloped by this "being of light," who asked: "Will you go? Will you tend my sheep?"

"And here I am," she says with a seasoned chuckle.

Not long after that experience, she visited her father in Berkeley, California, where he served as minister at the University Christian Church. "I knew I was done in Cincinnati, but I didn't know what the next steps were," Chris continues. "While visiting my Dad, I figured them out. He and I talked at length about all that I had been going through. He was a great help to me in discerning that perhaps God was calling me into ordained ministry."

Ultimately, Chris attended the Pacific School of Religion, an interdenominational seminary across the street from her father's church. "It meant that I would need to move from Cincinnati to California, which I was not unhappy to do," says Chris, who began her studies in the winter of 1977.

"I had come out to my parents the summer between my sophomore and junior years of college," she continues. "They weren't thrilled, but neither were they condemning. That my being a lesbian would be a problem to them—or to the church—never occurred to me. That's how unscathed I was by my faith tradition."

During the ordination process, however, Chris faced the real world. "I was out [of the closet] while attending seminary," she says. "In the late seventies and early eighties, that was miraculous, too. However, it was one thing to be an out student at the seminary. It was quite another to be an out candidate for ordination. We all struggled with what it meant for me to seek ordination as an out lesbian. It was a wise decision on the part of the Ordination Commission to ask me to wait a year to be ordained following my graduation from seminary. The delay gave the leadership time to ask the Region to consider adding a clause to their guidelines for ordination."

The clause stated that "no single, arbitrary human condition will automatically bar a qualified candidate from the ordination process." At the 1980 Regional Assembly, the resolution was adopted by a vote of sixty-five to forty. "In April 1981, I was presented to the Regional Assembly as a candidate worthy of ordination," she says. "I was ordained at the University Christian Church on May 3, 1981. The love, blessings, and validation I received that day continue to be a source of strength and affirmation for me."

That winter, Chris applied for an associate minister's position in a church near Knoxville, Tennessee. "The congregation welcomed me with open arms," she recalls. "I was going to serve as the associate minister as well as the minister of music. At the close of the three days I spent there, the contract was presented for my signature. I took courage in hand and told the pastor—who had been a seminary classmate of my father—that I'm a lesbian. I made that disclosure because I trusted him and wanted no secrets between us. With that, he took the contract away from me before I had a chance to sign it."

"You might as well have shot yourself," he said, then phoned the chair of the search committee to tell him that Chris had turned down their call.

"I was devastated and confused by this turn of events," Chris continues. "I returned to California and submitted my application to the Clinical Pastoral Education program at St. Elizabeth's Hospital in Washington, D.C. God was good to me. I was accepted into the internship program. In May, following my ordination, I moved to Washington. The additional education and experience in ministry was critical to my professional and personal growth. Things could not have turned out better for me."

In 1982, Chris moved to New York City, primarily because she had fallen in love with a woman who worked and lived there. In New York, Chris worked as hospital chaplain and as a hospice chaplain in New Jersey. Through her hospice work she met Randy, the senior minister of the Glen Ridge Congregational Church.

In 1984, he invited her to apply for the associate minister's position. "He didn't know about my sexual orientation at the time, and I wasn't about to tell him after what happened to me in Tennessee," she explains. "I really wanted to work in a local church. I saw this as my only opportunity. The search committee unanimously offered me the position, and I accepted."

As part of the package, the church provided Chris a big house to live in. "The night I negotiated the contract, I told the search committee that I didn't want to live by myself, and knew several people who would be willing to room with me and make a monthly donation to the church," she says. "They agreed. Of course, the person I picked was Barbara, my partner at the time." Chris chuckles. "Bless their hearts. Some got it, and some didn't."

Finally, Chris told Randy of her sexual orientation. "I had to; I couldn't stand the secrecy between us," she explains. "I knew he would figure it out at some point, and I dreaded being confronted with the inevitable question: 'Why didn't you tell me before you were hired?' I assured him I would never, ever do anything to cause a schism in the congregation. Randy was not angry—just surprised. He had no regrets about hiring me; he even thanked me for my honesty."

Ultimately, Chris's presence was great for the parishioners, but terrible for her. "The duplicity gnawed at me every day," she explains. "I lived in terror that I would be 'outed' to the congregation and forced to resign in order to keep my promise not to cause a schism. Unable to say who I was, and who Barbara was to me, our relationship suffocated to death by the spring of

1986. Following our separation, I was grieving and hurting; I could not tell people in the congregation what was going on. It was a very dark time. Finally, I resigned in 1987, after a year of living alone in the parsonage and struggling with how to have a personal life and be in the ministry."

Chris has not worked in a local congregation since.

Coming out—and staying out—has been an arduous journey for Chris. "Coming out has been a process of learning how to integrate who I am with what I am," she explains. "The outside 'me' finally matches the inside 'me.' There is no more duplicity. It means that I can live from the inside out, rather than the outside in. I much prefer 'firsthand' life to a 'secondhand' one. For those of us who are gay and lesbian, coming out is an amazing catalyst for emotional and spiritual growth. The more I have developed a firsthand faith in God, the more I have developed a firsthand faith in myself as a lesbian who is a Christian minister."

Where is Chris now in her journey? "I am happy to say that I am able to use much of what I have learned and experienced to help other gay and lesbian people simply do what I have already done," she says. "It's very meaningful to me that I am doing what God called me to do. I am tending Her sheep—straight and gay alike. When I am visibly and verbally out about being lesbian and Christian, I am not just a role model for gay and lesbian people. I am impacting straight people, too—people who need to experience someone like me. I can't think of a better way to help others grapple and grow so they can be healed of their confusion and homophobia."

Exiling churches perpetrate shame and duplicity by "accepting" gay and lesbian clergy only when they remain in the closet, pledge celibacy, or pretend to be heterosexual. When ministers cannot serve with honesty and integrity—when their efforts at self-preservation impede a forthright delivery of God's message—they cannot effectively lead congregations to spiritual maturity. As witnesses in exile, their voices are hollow. Their parishioners hear them only from a distant place—a less-than-honest place. God's message is limited. Congregations are shortchanged.

However, gay and lesbian clergy who affirm the fullness of their humanity take a tremendous risk. Congregations may see them through the distortions of stereotype and prejudice—perhaps even hatred. Ultimately, they may be forced to abandon the church they love so much.

But other ministers break out of the clerical closet amid tumult, hostility, even humiliation. They refuse to leave those faith traditions that once embraced them as men and women of spiritual merit.

They stay. But at what price—and why?

3

PROPHETS AMID TUMULT

Can God Do a New Thing?

In mainline traditions today, a perilous dichotomy prevails. Church officials invariably assert their commitment to prayerful dialog about inclusion of homosexual parishioners and the ordination of homosexual clergy. At the same time, church members who come out are often ostracized or subjected to the brutal rhetoric drawn from the arsenal of the Religious Right. Ministers who come out greatly risk losing their pulpits. When Doug Nissing, an Episcopal priest in Connecticut, told a congregation that he was gay, he received a phone call saying some members had a problem with hiring a gay priest. As a result, they would not offer him a job (*Fairfield County Weekly,* Stamford, Connecticut, 1998). Now, because of his honesty, the possibility of a career inside the Episcopal Diocese of Connecticut has been closed, because the diocese has taken a rigid stance against allowing gays and lesbians to hold positions of leadership within the church. "If I wanted to go back to a parish ministry," Nissing, who now works as a full-time therapist, told Robert Nixon, "I would have to go somewhere outside the state of Connecticut."

Martha Dyson's journey toward honesty with herself and others began with the question, What kind of crazy God would call a lesbian to be a priest? As noted in Chapter 2, Martha was ordained an Episcopal priest in April 1994. She has served St. Paul's Cathedral in Burlington, Vermont, since February 1997. "I got involved in fundamentalism when I was about seventeen," she begins. "I did street ministry with an organization called the Agape Force. Eventually, I left them because they were so rigid and didn't allow for questions. The organization wasn't a cult, but it had cultish behavior. Their emphasis was on conformity and listening to authorities. After that experience, I continued for a while in the framework of fundamentalism because I desperately wanted religion to be simple. Finally, a part of me said it was too simple. I realized fundamentalism is really a house of cards. The whole thing falls apart eventually. If someone asks you to remove just one card, you can't accept that, because acceptance would mean all the cards fall down."

In 1984, Martha felt a strong desire to study theology. At the time, because of her love of studying and teaching, she intended to become a professor. "I went to Oral Roberts University to study the Bible," she says. "While there,

I went through a dramatic transformation. The experience opened me up to things I had not known and questioned before. My fundamentalist structure began to collapse."

At Oral Roberts University, a 200-foot-tall futuristic Prayer Tower stands, like an extraterrestrial spacecraft, in the center of campus. Inside the structure, a cadre of telephone operators takes prayer requests, while an eternal flame atop the tower evokes either awe or disdain from campus visitors. That any student would be encouraged to question scripture might be met with skepticism. "The university is conservative, it's true," Martha concedes. "But at least when I attended, the professors were not biblical literalists. Instead, they had a high view of scripture. Still, I was pretty much within that fundamentalist system while studying there."

Slowly, however, Martha's world began to change. "During my years at ORU, my fundamentalism fell apart, and I became disillusioned with the Assemblies of God tradition," she continues. "I had met, and fallen in love with, another woman who was also studying at Oral Roberts University. Together, we began attending an Episcopal Church. Before I met her, I was not conscious of my lesbianism. I knew I was always drawn to women, but it never occurred to me that it was a sexual thing. Unfortunately, this woman was conflicted about whether what was happening to us was right. I shared that sense of conflict, which created a split between what I thought and what I felt."

Soon, the two women broke up, creating questions for Martha about the reality of her orientation. She began her doctorate work at Drew University, convinced once again that she would ultimately earn a university professorship. "But people began asking if I wanted to be ordained," she explains. "My reaction was 'no way.' What kind of crazy God would call a lesbian to be a priest?"

Because of her enrollment at Drew, Martha located in the most progressive diocese of Newark, New Jersey—the diocese of John Shelby Spong—where her interest in ordination began. "I struggled even then with the idea of whether I should come out. Even though Dr. Spong was a real supporter, I went through the process [of ordination] with the idea that I'm not going in, blazing guns, with the announcement that I'm lesbian."

However, during a weekend retreat for ordination candidates, the topic of sexual orientation arose. Martha responded honestly to the inevitable questions. "What was wonderfully affirming was their unanimous acceptance of me," she recalls. "I had worked so hard on coming out that there was no way I could go back [into the closet]."

In 1991, Martha, as a seminarian, was assigned to the Church of the Redeemer in Morristown, New Jersey. "The congregation was on the cutting edge in terms of inclusive language liturgies. They were also welcoming to gays and lesbians. But I was still concerned about how out I could really be and still get ordained. I'd originally intended to come out very cautiously, but that's not what ended up happening. Every week I looked out over the congregation and saw so many gay and lesbian people looking back at me, and I thought, 'How can I stand up here in the pulpit and have integrity if I'm not being fully honest about who I am?' Being a part of that wonderful congregation was a significant part of my coming-out process. They treated me as a healthy, normal human being and that enabled me to see myself that way, too."

In 1993, Martha met Chris Leslie (see Chapter 2); they had committed to each other as partners by 1994, when Martha officially became an Episcopal priest. "Chris was introduced as my partner during my ordination ceremony," Martha says. "However, I didn't immediately look for a church job. By the middle of 1994, I accepted a job working at an HIV outpatient clinic. I did that for more than two years. I also did supply pastoring for Episcopal churches around the diocese."

Soon, Martha heard of a vacancy at St. Paul's Cathedral in Burlington, Vermont. After acquiring assurances of Chris's willingness to relocate, Martha called to speak to the rector about the position.

"How do you think the congregation feels about welcoming gays and lesbians?" she asked.

"I'm not exactly sure I can answer that," he said. "But I don't think it would be an issue in hiring."

"I want to be up-front from the beginning," Martha replied. "I'm a lesbian. I can't be a minister and return to the closet. I have to be honest."

Shortly after their conversation the rector sent a set of questions for Martha to answer. Soon after, she sent the congregation a sample sermon. Finally, the selection pool narrowed, leaving only Martha and one other candidate for consideration. "I came up from New Jersey and met with the three people on the search committee," Martha continues. "The interview for assistant rector went well. Finally, I got a call, stating that I was still the church's candidate of choice."

"You're still the person we're interested in," the rector said. "Now we need to see if the vestry thinks the congregation can handle having an out lesbian as their priest."

A few days later, the rector called. Sure enough, the vestry wanted to meet her. "Chris and I came back to Vermont and attended both worship services that Sunday morning," Martha says. "We also attended adult education classes. I put everything on the table."

Martha told parishioners that she was not interested in being a minister to the gay and lesbian community alone; that's why she had chosen to pursue a pulpit in a mainline congregation. "We had a friendly conversation. It was important for them to meet Martha Dyson, the human being, not Martha Dyson, the lesbian. I felt everything had gone really well."

Then, the rector called. "I could tell something was wrong," Martha admits. "I'm really sorry," he said. "I don't think we're going to be able to do this."

Martha was shocked. "What happened?" she asked. "Things seemed to be going so well."

He sighed. "Well, I just had several conversations with some people in the congregation," the rector said. "It will be too big of a shift."

Martha was stunned.

"I'm sorry," the rector said quietly.

Martha hung up. She desperately needed someone to talk to. Because Chris wasn't home, she called several other clergy friends. "We hung out together, trying to process what had happened," Martha says.

Three hours later, the phone rang again. Martha was surprised to hear the rector's voice. "I've made a terrible mistake," he said. "Please come."

"What happened?" Martha asked. "Why such a dramatic shift in such a short time?"

The rector launched into an explanation. "Over the past couple of hours, I called other vestry members who were surprised and shocked by my conclusion," he said. "You see, I allowed a few people with prejudices and fears about homosexuality to sway my view. There is enough support among church leaders that they feel they can handle any fears and concerns the congregation might have."

Finally, Martha was able to speak. "Well, I'm stunned right now," she said. "I need a little time to process—everything."

As Martha discussed the telephone conversation with both partner and friends, she concluded that she needed to know whether the rector intended to educate the congregation about gay and lesbian issues. She could not bear the thought of serving as assistant rector in a hostile environment.

"Okay, here's the situation," Martha said when he called again the next morning. "I need to know that I can trust you."

"I hear that," he replied. "And yes, you can trust me."

When Martha joined the ministerial staff, several members of the congregation left, "but there was no huge exit. Most parishioners have been okay with my orientation; others have never been okay, but they are the minority. Still others don't even process it; I'm their priest, so my sexuality doesn't enter into the equation."

Although she has made references to her partnership with Chris and to homosexuality in sermons, Martha has never used homosexuality as the premise for a sermon at St. Paul's. "Part of my reasoning is that simply by my being here, and being out—well, that's affirmation enough," she explains. "I want people to know me. I don't regard the pulpit as an ever-present opportunity to express my opinions about gay and lesbian issues. However, in my sermons, I focus on the fact that all people are welcome at the table. I do talk freely in those terms. There's not an in or out crowd."

One evening, a married heterosexual couple in their eighties invited Martha and Chris to their home for dinner. "I noticed Chris was in the paper recently," the woman said as she set the table. "There's such a lovely picture of her. Would you like to have another copy?"

"That's representative of the acceptance level I enjoy at the church," Martha says. "There's nothing confrontational about my relationship with the congregation."

Martha's position of comfort in her openness has freed other gay and lesbian parishioners to come out more confidently. "Recently, we had a welcoming service when about twenty people joined our church," she recalls. "Two of those people were lesbian partners. Our bulletin listed them as a couple."

Ironically, when gays and lesbians establish committed partnerships, many heterosexual Christians experience their greatest sense of trepidation. Martha regards their discomfort as a result of the misinformation disseminated by Christian thinkers of past eras. "First of all, sexuality has to do with embodiment," Martha says. "We are not spirits, just floating around. Our bodies are not just *part* of who we are—they *are* us. Christianity has struggled with this fact for eons. Sexuality is one of the most intimate embodied experiences that a human being can have. In my view, it shouldn't be taken lightly or without reverence. There is no shame in it, whether it's heterosexual or homosexual in nature. Pleasure is good, because pleasure is one of God's gifts. Sexuality is a good thing when it is treated with care and respect. Spirituality and sexuality are innately intertwined. We've got to get over this damaging attitude that the body is somehow evil."

Same-sex marriage is an issue Martha strongly supports. "We're talking about a spiritual connection between two people," she explains. "And we're talking about legalities. On both counts, marriage is a good thing. It's not for everybody, and I don't think people, regardless of orientation, should feel forced into it. However, I will be first in line when it's legal. Chris and I are active members of the task force [on legalizing same-sex marriage in Vermont]. We know one of the three couples who are part of the lawsuit. It's time for this particular configuration of family to get the breaks."

During years of training, of prayer, of soul searching prior to turning herself over to the ministry, Martha's desire to know the truth about spirituality, about Christianity, forced her to open herself to ideas that were often uncomfortable. In her view, no Christian is exempt from the discomfort and excitement of new learning. "God is not going to be threatened by the truth," she says. "And neither should we. What it comes down to, in the long run, is that ministers have to help people overcome their fear of the truth. Many Christians who don't recognize or acknowledge their gay and lesbian brothers and sisters clearly have chinks in their armor. Despite their rhetoric of opposition, they're longing to know the truth. We must help these people ask themselves: 'If I have to close my ears to new information, then what kind of God am I protecting?'"

Many sympathetic mainline Christians wonder how churches can purport a desire for dialog when gay and lesbian church leaders stand to lose so much. Although churches occasionally declare periods of prayer and reflection, rather than discussions of homosexuality—the Episcopal, Lutheran, and Presbyterian faith traditions have all attempted to silence the voices of dissent so "other business can be done"—they are often unrestrained in chastising or even dismissing gay and lesbian pastors who find leading celibate lives unconscionable. Often, church officials discount a congregation's respect for their gay and lesbian pastors once violations of church policy are charged. As a result, parishioners find themselves caught uncomfortably in the middle. They feel strong commitment to their spiritual leaders; they mourn the possibility of losing them. Simultaneously, they know a church hierarchy's verdict of guilt could translate into the loss of their church—if they choose to keep their pastor in defiance of church rulings.

Most mainline denominations tolerate single gay and lesbian pastors who remain celibate, though the silence and patronization resulting from tolerance create distance between clergy and parishioners. However, if falling in love compels ministers to commit themselves to a partner, church officials can—and often do—invoke charges of policy violation against these pastors. From the perspective of gay and lesbian ministers, and their justice-seeking allies, defrocking clergy who maintain a committed, monogamous relationship with a same-sex partner exposes a disturbing double standard. What's okay for straight ministers is unacceptable for gay and lesbian colleagues. For heterosexual church officials and members of the denomination adhering to a traditional biblical standard of human sexuality, the pastor gets what he or she deserves.

Without exception, once an "offending" minister is charged, the argument arises that church policy or denominational guidelines of faith stipulate ordination only for a minister who is single and celibate, or who is married. The argument's obvious catch-22 is that marriage is reserved exclusively for heterosexual couples. Therefore, options for same-sex couples are limited. Either they live apart with clandestine encounters outside (or within) the parsonage, or they live together outside the bounds of holy matrimony. Most gay and lesbian ministers assert that, with their denomination's approval, they would choose to marry their partners.[1]

Another disturbing component of the ordination controversy is the persistent demonization of homosexuality. In the view of many church officials—though their numbers are decreasing—gays and lesbians lack common sense, decency, and integrity, lead hedonistic lives, or suffer from an "intrinsic moral disorder." Often, heterosexuals experiencing no empathy with a gay man or lesbian woman—or having no understanding of their capacity for love and commitment—are willing to testify against gay and lesbian clergy in a church trial, citing in repressively stereotypical terms the moral inferiority of homosexuality. Laity cannot possibly imagine the effects of such arguments on ministers who possess intrinsic knowledge of their spiritual integrity, and at heart sense that their committed relationships are virtuous and honorable. Regardless of the outcome of church proceedings on charges of disobedience or violation of church policy, accused ministers feel betrayed by a denomination that has led them—and their congregations—to believe that gay and lesbian Christians are embraced by their communities of worship. Steve Sabin, for example, was found guilty of violating the policy of the Evangelical Lutheran Church in America because of his long-term relationship with his partner. The denomination's hierarchy told him to leave his church, despite his congregation's full acceptance of him. "This don't-ask-don't-tell policy doesn't serve anyone's interest," says Steve. "It fosters psychological dysfunction and does not serve the best interest of the church."

In London, England, where more than seven hundred Episcopal bishops from churches around the world gathered in 1998 for the once-a-decade Lambeth Conference, a group of lesbian and gay Christians appealed for a "healthy debate" on their place in the Episcopal Church USA, which is sharply divided over the issue of homosexuality. Although conservative factions periodically arise, Episcopal bishops frequently ordain gays and lesbians, and priests perform commitment ceremonies for same-sex couples. However, despite the Episcopal Church's reputation for progressivism, church officials and parishioners are by no means united in their view of homosexuality. In fact, Archbishop of Canterbury George Carey, leader of the Conference, urged more study. "I said . . . last year that I see no justification from scripture, nor from the entire Christian tradition, for a break away from what we've inherited: sexuality expressed in marriage, and celibacy outside marriage."[2] In other words, gay and lesbian priests with partners could expect—officially, at least—little relief from the duplicitous nature of serving the Episcopal Church.

In the United States, a Burning Issues conference held in Richmond, Virginia (December 1997) dramatized the rift in the Episcopal conscience.[3] According to Doug LeBlanc, "the right relies on propositional truth and often abstract principles, while the left appeals to people's emotions through powerful storytelling and firsthand experience." LeBlanc framed the issues in bellicose images—those who support ordination of clergy of both orientations and inclusion against those determined to uphold the status quo. As a result, conservative Episcopalians face a "daunting challenge" to win others to their point of view. To gather more conservatives into the fold, they must learn more effective storytelling techniques. LeBlanc contends that stories of gay men and lesbians who have suffered discrimination and even hatred at the hands of bigots make more of an impact than conservative theological arguments. "For now, our arguments are not moving people to tears," he says.

"This may not be a truth we want to face, but in today's Episcopal Church, that means losing not only the hearts, but also the votes at Convention, of our fellow Episcopalians."

The controversy over homosexual ordination has continued in the Episcopal Church since 1979, when the ECUSA determined that the ordination of celibate homosexuals would be permitted. Although the traditional policy forbids ordination of "practicing" homosexuals, the policy has never been enshrined in canon law. In fact, since 1979, over one hundred gay men and lesbians have been ordained as Episcopal priests and deacons in the United States.[4]

At several conventions hosted during the eighties, the Episcopal Church established commissions to study more effective ways to minister to the needs of gays and lesbians. However, during the nineties, or "The Decade of Evangelism," "we seem intent on alienating and keeping out one of the few identifiable groups of people who want to be welcomed in," concluded the 1992 Standing Commission on Human Affairs. In 1994, the controversial Bishop John Shelby Spong, who ordained several gay and lesbian priests during his service to the Newark, New Jersey, diocese, issued a statement that "homosexual persons who choose to live out their sexual orientation in a partnership that is marked by faithfulness and life-giving holiness" should be eligible for ordination. Seventy-two other bishops signed the statement. In 1996, Anglican Archbishop of South Africa Desmond Tutu wrote the foreword to a book of lesbian and gay-affirming church liturgies stating that "we reject [homosexuals] . . . as pariahs, and push them outside our church communities, and thereby we negate the consequences of their baptism and ours. We make them doubt that they are the children of God, and this must be nearly the ultimate blasphemy. We blame them for something that is becoming increasingly clear they can do little about."[5]

However, a vociferous conservative wing always responds quickly. During a bishop's trial for heresy (Walter C. Righter, a heterosexual, ordained an openly gay priest living in a committed, ten-year relationship), the right wing of the Episcopal Church clearly initiated "the ecclesiastical version of 'ethnic cleansing.'" The ten bishops who brought the heresy charges against Bishop Righter "proposed to give the 1997 General Convention the opportunity to affirm its acceptance of the authority of Holy Scripture that this court has refused to accept." That refusal came in the form of dismissal of all charges.[6]

Advocates of stripping the denomination of its "progressive reputation" also expressed trepidation over the common perception of the Episcopal Church as "a denomination recognized for blessing same-sex unions, ordaining actively gay and lesbian persons, and attempting to re-write the *Book of Common Prayer*," according to the Episcopal Laity Group.[7] Members of the Group also ran full-page ads in four state newspapers, accusing the Episcopal Church of attempting to "replace biblical truth and godly morality with secular humanism and moral relativism." "We scratch where we itch, and even the most casual observer of the Episcopal Church knows that homosexuality is where we itch," writes R. R. Reno.[8] Entire congregations have left the Episcopal Church to join other denominations, or to become independent, because of where the Episcopal Church "itches."[9]

In local parishes, priests expressed dismay that the Episcopal Church houses two different religions "under one roof." Conservatives were concerned that the General Convention, committed to the continuation of a "study" of the blessing of gay and lesbian partnerships, allowed dioceses to extend insurance coverage to domestic partners of its employees. Acceptance of homosexuality is "just one more step in the erosion of Christian morality in the Episcopal Church," says David Moyer, rector of Good Shepherd parish in Rosemont, Pennsylvania. (Moyer also opposes the ordination of women.) "Church doctrine says either engage in married heterosexuality or lead a chaste life, but the diocese seems to think the established biblical historical doctrines of the church are no longer applicable. . . . How can I now lecture young people and tell them my diocese says fornication and sodomy are not to be avoided?"[10]

Less conservative ministers view the Convention's willingness to study the issues as part of Christianity's evolution. "If I quote the Old Testament in terms of same-gender sexual expression, I can also say slavery is okay, masturbation is sinful, [having] multiple wives is okay. So we can't develop Christian moral codes purely on the moral codes of the first century and before." What Christians need to ask themselves, according to Rev. Ruth L. Kirk, is whether "God can do a new thing. And can God use the church to do a new thing?" In January 1998, Bishop Frank T. Griswold was installed as the Episcopal Church's presiding bishop. Considered a centrist within the denomination, Bishop Griswold signed a statement in 1994 that sexual orientation is "morally neutral" and that "faithful, monogamous, committed" gay and lesbian relationships should be accepted. "It is important to realize," he said, "that contemporary understanding of human sexuality is much more advanced than it was in biblical times."[11]

A Demeaning Tolerance

During a period of seven years, Michael Hopkins' congregation has grown in size from about thirty members to one hundred twenty-five. "And I've been out from the beginning," the Episcopal priest says. "I was one of five candidates sent to the church as a selection pool. I think what biased the selection committee was that my partner at the time was serving as interim priest. They had experienced him for a year, knew he was gay, and liked him very much. After a few weeks of struggling, they decided to give me a chance. One-fifth of the congregation's members defected because of my selection—including some church leaders. Actually, their departure gave the church a chance to have a new life."

Michael serves a parish in Maryland, just outside Washington, D.C. He estimates that about 15 percent of his parishioners are gay or lesbian—a fact that doesn't bother the other 85 percent. "It's also no big deal that I've been partnered for six years," Michael adds. "My congregation was so comfortable with me, they accepted John very readily." In fact, his parish helped the two men with the down payment for the house they purchased in 1995.

Michael concedes that pockets of fundamentalism exist within the Episcopal Church, but "generally speaking, the trend is in the other direction. Dioceses have taken stances contrary to my own diocese, where my leadership is especially careful to keep track of John and me, to see how well we're doing, and to make sure we have enough quality time together. Even so, my bishop is not yet supportive of commitment ceremonies between same-sex partners" that occur in Michael's diocese, although he looks the other way as long as no controversy erupts.

In seminary, Michael, along with several other seminarians, "forced the [homosexual] issues a little. That was in the mid-eighties. My professors told me that because I was out, I would most likely never be a parish priest. I would have to find other ways to exercise my ministry. I realize now they were trying to make sure I was being realistic. Now, things have changed a great deal, and there is a lot more public conversation about the issues."

But when Michael first came out, a closeted seminary professor "explained to my partner and me how to keep quiet in the church—how to survive and not make waves," Michael relates, recalling his first year of ministry. "In that small community, keeping quiet would have meant not living together. We would have been forced to maintain a long-distance relationship."

From Michael's perspective, attitudes found in various faith communities have taken a tremendous toll on gay and lesbian Christians. "Gay and lesbian people are often raised to believe there is a split between sexuality and spirituality," he explains. "So many have been forced by their churches to choose between the two—be sexual, or be spiritual. That is a horrible divide with which to confront *anyone.*"

Michael understands the leeriness and hostility some gay men and lesbians feel toward religious institutions. "The church deserves it," he says, "and has done lots to deserve it. I *try* to offer gays and lesbians a way into the church." He chuckles. "As I share my spiritual experiences, they often can't get away from me fast enough. Churches could provide so much stability in a world that is not particularly supportive of us. Our relationships do not have structure that the church *could* provide. I perform commitment ceremonies. My congregation treats John and me as they would any married couple. But the paradise we've found isn't true of most faith communities."

Indeed, in some regions of the United States, even the progressive Episcopal tradition fails to provide anything close to paradise. Harry Scott Coverston, ordained in 1995, cannot answer his call to minister in the Florida diocese. "Here, in Orlando, the bishop will not permit a gay priest to serve in his parishes," he explains. "So I am excluded from ministering in the diocese in which I have lived most of my life. One must either be married or celibate here, which, in the latter case, is perfectly honorable so long as it is a voluntary vocation discerned by the individual and God and honored by the church. The attempts of the church to impose such a vocation, however, is both misguided and destructive. It also draws a bead on the hypocrisy of a church that, on the one hand, refuses to marry same-sex couples, then penalizes those who live in relationships other than marriage. [Before I was accepted by the seminary, my homosexuality] served as a personal response to the little whispering voice inside that spoke of ordination—'I can't seek orders; I'm gay.' When it became clear that my homosexuality might not be an impediment if I left home to seek orders elsewhere, I had no excuses. That was the point I closed my law practice, quit my college teaching job, packed my Mazda 323 to the ceiling, kissed my partner and family good-by and drove across the continent to Berkeley."

The closet has had a stultifying effect on Harry's ministry. "I often have to carefully gauge how I phrase something," he explains. "I have to be aware of who I am talking with at all times. It has always been clear that I could not be myself in most contexts. This was particularly true of my ministry as a deacon in a middle class white parish in Hayward, California, and of my assistant chaplaincy work at the Chapel of the Resurrection at Florida State University. For the most part, I've had to keep my personal life, my partnership of twenty-four years, and my 'real self' to myself. I find it unconscionable that the church would require anyone to live a lie, particularly its leaders."

Furthermore, gay and lesbian parishoners are dehumanized by the intersection of their lives with mainline denominational attitudes. "As I studied and prayed and grew in the parish that presented me for ordination—a multicultural parish in San Jose, California—I began to realize one thing," he explains. "Not only is tolerance *not enough;* it is also demeaning. This realization occurred to me in a parish where I was out, and where my partner and I were always seen as a partnered couple and treated with the same dignity married couples were treated. But tolerance always operates out of a condescension on the part of a supposed superior to an alleged inferior. That is not the stuff of loving relationships; it is a power relationship, and one that I increasingly became aware that the gospel simply couldn't countenance, much less legitimate."

Harry experienced yet another shift in consciousness after attending three General Conventions. "I began to consider the patterns of the rhetoric of the Episcopal Church around sexuality issues," he says. "What disturbed me was the way that the role of gays and lesbians was almost always analyzed in terms of rights. But the arguments usually went something to the effect that such rights should be extended to gays and lesbians because it was the right thing to do—very much in terms of *noblesse oblige,* white man's burden, a sad legacy of the Episcopal Church's traditional role as the church of the upper middle class."

It was a point of reference with which Harry could not agree. "The more I came to see myself as a child of God, created very good though imperfect, and thus just as entitled to all the sacraments and offices of the church as a straight person by virtue of being a child of God, the more I began to see that extension of rights was not the right approach," he continues. "What the Episcopal Church needed to come to grips with was the reality that a benefit enjoyed by some of its members and not others was not a right but a privilege. Dismantling the arbitrary barriers which protected that privilege was something the church needed to do for its own good, for the sake of its own soul. Its own integrity was in jeopardy—[as was] every baptism when the baptismal covenant was recited by the members assembled. Its veracity was in question every time the congregation recited the second of the Great Commandments. The church was doing gays and lesbians no favors in the process of dismantling systems of heterosexist privilege. It was doing what was right and, in the process, addressing a wrongful practice it had been engaged in for centuries."

Being a gay minister has also made Harry accessible to other marginalized Episcopalians. "Many women have found me an easy man to approach—including one woman who has been able to discuss some rather horrific sexual abuse as a child," he explains. "I have been present for young gay men coming to the realization of their sexuality in a pastoral manner that was, sadly, not present for me when I came out. It is a blessing and a curse, I think."

Another blessing of Harry's life occurred during his ordination and contrasts dramatically to the bishop's attitude in Central Florida.

"No one gets through this process alone," Harry's bishop announced at his ordination. "Every candidate has someone to help him or her on the road to ordination. In Harry's life, that someone has been his partner, Andy. I want Andy to join Harry up front. Let us show Andy our appreciation for his role in this process."

"We got a standing ovation," Harry says quietly.

But ordination does not guarantee a minister's assignment to a parish, where the messages are often muddled. "On the one hand, we have a canon law provision that says no one may be denied admission to the process for ordination due to sexual orientation," Harry explains. "But obviously, admission to the process does *not* mean ordination will result or, of more importance, that deployment to a parish, mission, special ministry, or chaplaincy will result. Episcopal bishops essentially have what amounts to local option, and thus ordination practices vary from diocese to diocese like a patchwork quilt. On the other hand, the policy-making General Convention has repeatedly turned back attempts to prohibit gay and lesbian ordinations, and came within a single vote of making it possible to bless unions last convention. Given the direction of convention voting patterns, most observers within the church believe the unions measure will pass in two years."

However, decisions of the General Convention do not translate into attitudinal changes on the level where they count most. "I am eager to remove the last vestiges of heterosexism within the church and get on with the business of being a church for all God's people—a church whose signs out front and on the edge of town can accurately advertise that they 'WELCOME YOU' regardless of who you are. On the other hand, I realize that the attitudes that feed this heterosexism are the product of centuries of practice and development. They did not arise in a short time, and they won't be addressed in a short time—not in any effective manner. My stance is that if we don't intend to ordain homosexuals or bless their unions, we shouldn't baptize them either."

To many students of Christianity, the Episcopal Church is known as "the church of the refugee." The description doesn't apply to the Orlando diocese. "Here, a remarkable role reversal has occurred in which the local Roman Catholic diocese has made public reconciling gestures and is operating a gay and lesbian ministry [in Orlando]," Harry says. "The ECUSA diocese has driven gay and lesbian parishioners out and refuses to let Integrity [an organization of gay and lesbian Episcopalians and their friends who call the ECUSA to include lesbians and gay men fully in the life of the Episcopal Church] meet in any parish. The parish I attend from time to time is moderately welcoming and has two closeted gay priests on its staff. Another parish has a monthly evensong it advertises in the local gay newspaper. But these are the rare exceptions."

Gay and lesbian Christians should speak out loudly and persistently against religious bigotry, Harry believes, whenever it is used to exclude them from faith communities. "No one owns the church," Harry says. "No one speaks exclusively for God. No one has exclusive rights to interpret scripture. Gays and lesbians should *never* assume that they must respond defensively regarding Christianity. We are the children of God, bearing the divine image just like the next person. By dismissing the faith as irrelevant to our lives and focusing on politics, we essentially offer no resistance within the church to a rather mindless and superficial appropriation of scripture and tradition by folks with no more inherent claim to those commodities than the next person, including gays and lesbians."

As long as he lives in Orlando, Harry doubts he will ever be allowed to serve as a priest again. "Likely, I will make my living teaching," he says. "Unless there is a major unexpected change in this diocese, that essentially means I will not function as a priest until Andy and I move somewhere else. The main repercussion of being out and being ordained is that if you are not living in the dioceses where such a combination is consistent with serving the church, you don't serve. Other dioceses have also passed restrictive provisions. If a clergy person runs afoul of those provisions, the bishop could suspend him or her. More likely, however, is a revolt at the parish level that would ultimately spell the end of one's tenure."

The 1998 Lambeth Conference might have made running afoul of church provisions significantly easier when it passed a resolution that homosexual relations are "incompatible with scripture," and priesthood should be off-limits to gays and lesbians. Although the Episcopal Church USA may eventually "do a new thing," progressive American bishops were outnumbered by a margin of 526–70, with forty-five bishops abstaining.[12]

Immediately following the Conference, Washington Bishop Ronald Haines issued an apology to gay and lesbian parishioners in the Episcopal Church, and pledged that its bishops would "continue to reflect, pray and work for your full inclusion in the life of the Church."

Yet inclusion without controversy may still be a long time coming in the Episcopal Church and other mainline denominations, as many church hierarchies muzzle debate over homosexual ordination until a time when argument might be less inflammatory. "Not since slavery . . . has there been an issue that has as much potential to divide religious communities as this one," said Barbara Wheeler, president of Auburn Presbyterian Theological Seminary in New York.[13]

Creating a Big Sin

Although the Lambeth Conference shocked American Episcopalians with its denunciation of homosexual clergy, nowhere has the noise over the issue of ordination of gay and lesbian ministers been louder than within the Presbyterian Church (U.S.A.) [PC(USA)]. Since 1978, the denomination has stuck to its sanctions against the ordination of "self-affirming" homosexuals. In recent years, however, sentiment has grown more sympathetic toward capable gay and lesbian clergy who regard unilateral celibacy vows as double standards—but not sympathetic enough to facilitate any official policy changes.

In 1996, as advocates for homosexual ordination expressed outrage and surprise, the General Assembly passed Policy G-6.0106b, simply called Amendment B. It states: "Those who are called to office in the church are to lead a life in obedience to Jesus Christ, under the authority of the Scripture and in conformity to the historic confessional standards of the church. Among these standards is the requirement to live either in fidelity within the covenant of marriage between a man and a woman, or chastity in singleness. Persons refusing to repent of any self-acknowledged practice which the confessions call sin shall not be ordained and/or installed as deacons, elders, or ministers of the Word and Sacrament."

Once the General Assembly convened in 1998, overtures were made to strike the "fidelity and chastity" amendment from the *Book of Common*

Prayer and replace it with "fidelity and integrity in marriage or singleness, and in all relationships of life," supplanting Amendment B with the revised Amendment A. Proponents did not succeed, and Amendment B remained in effect, but not without controversy. "We cannot live as a denomination if we have to resolve this one way or another," Rev. John Buchanan of Chicago stated prior to the defeat of the new amendment. "And in the long run, Amendment A gives us a better chance of holding together, of not driving people out of the church."[14]

But as debate heightened, moderates perceived the new amendment as an attempt to water down biblical standards on the question of human sexuality. Liberals did not understand their objections because they saw ordination of gays and lesbians, regardless of whether they commit themselves to celibacy or monogamy with a life partner, as an extension of their current beliefs to yet another marginalized community. However, the moderates didn't see such an action as "inclusive." Had Amendment A passed, they would have felt excluded and alienated because of their loyalty to traditional biblical exegesis.

"We are not saying that homosexuals cannot be members of the church, just that they can't be leaders," said Gretchen Huston, an elder at Southminster Presbyterian Church in Crestwood, Missouri.[15] "The church needs to speak out to our culture; it must not weaken marriage by allowing such leadership"—leadership that, according to Huston, would weaken family life in Presbyterian congregations. "If you don't protect the family, you end up with children growing up with one parent or sometimes no parents."

However, Jon Carroll, a Presbyterian writing for the *San Francisco Chronicle* ("Bad Cleric, No Cookie," March 23, 1998), felt such an argument camouflaged a less-than-honest agenda. "Look, if you want to discriminate against gay folks, say so," he writes. "Have the courage of your bigotry. Don't go sneaking around with bland defenses of the sacred marriage contract. Gay folks get married, too—in reality, if not in the Presbyterian Church. They take oaths and are serious about keeping them. They wish to serve in the worship of God in about the same numbers as straight people do." Carroll identified the bottom line as the Presbyterian Church's denigration of love. "Love is rare and unexpected," he continued. "We should be celebrating its appearance everywhere. We should not be taking its temperature, interrogating it in small rooms, asking it to describe its physical manifestations. When humans love humans, we are all enriched."

But like clergy in other mainline denominations, many Presbyterian ministers called for a moratorium on legislative and judicial measures dealing with human sexuality. That amounts to censorship, according to Laurene La-Fontaine, a Colorado minister and leader in the denomination's gay and lesbian movement. "The right wing wants to shut down debate because progress is being made," she alleges. "The church is scared of all this because it means people have to change. It means the acceptance of gays and lesbians. There is simply too much at stake in the lives of gay [and lesbian] Presbyterians and their families for us to even think about backing off from this long-term struggle for justice."[16]

On June 15, when Presbyterians gathered in Charlotte, North Carolina, for the 1998 General Assembly, they discovered that the call for a moratorium had been disregarded. "[I have] never borne the brunt of so much vicious mail than I did because of my support [last year] of Amendment A," said Robert W. Bohl, a former General Assembly moderator and co-moderator of the Covenant Network of Presbyterians. "We're the church. Remember that, and we will not allow ourselves to be victimized and villainized. . . . The issue here is not so much ordination standards as it is control, domination, and ultimately, the destruction of the church as we have known and loved it. We must not let this denomination become captive as the Southern Baptist Convention has become captive to those who systematically exclude and purge from leadership those who disagree with them."[17]

But for most gay and lesbian Presbyterian ministers, activism isn't an option in a climate that communicates that the Presbyterian Church has no idea how to regard its homosexual clergy. Like most mainline denominations, the PC(USA) would rather ignore the issues. As a result, the service of gay and lesbian Presbyterian ministers is delivered from the closet. Theologically, they share a vision of inclusiveness, compassion, and acceptance, but coming out would be a self-destructive request for trouble.

David Johnson first began to consider ministry in a mainline denomination while attending high school. "I grew up around a lot of fundamentalist friends," he says. "My church was more involved in social ministries than my friends' churches. I learned at this early age the differences in our understanding of Jesus and what his life and ministry meant to us. My friends were taught to be concerned about their personal salvation and 'getting themselves right' with God. This was never an issue in my church. We were just told we were saved, then pushed to show God's love to others out of gratitude for all we had."

Because of David's "intense need for social approval," he never considered the ramifications of homophobia and prejudice. "In high school, I was the best little boy in the world, so I did everything expected of me by my family and friends," he explains. "I was very popular, hung out with everyone, and never isolated anyone. I dated girls all through high school and college. But I was also aware that my most intense feelings were for other boys. I fell head over heels in love with one of my male junior high school teachers and got myself in detention just to be near him. On the other hand, I don't remember feeling the intense loneliness that other gays and lesbians often experience. Because of my need for social approval, I was able to 'turn off' my sexuality and conform to the straight way for a long time. I'm a very extroverted person and always made sure to have many friends, which limited the time I had to concentrate on my own innate orientation."

In David's opinion, a church's demands for duplicity are shameful. "After all, a high percentage of gays and lesbians enter the ministry because it attracts sensitive people," he explains. "In our society, many heterosexual men are not comfortable being vulnerable to others. They don't know how to be. By making us stay in the closet, the church really doesn't get the benefit of seeing all that we have to give and how loving many of our partnerships are. People think I'm just a happy, middle-aged bachelor. I seem so normal, but poor me—I never found a wife! My partner and I have been together for ten years. Our relationship is not perfect, but it's real. To not get that part of me, the church is really missing out—not to mention the pain such hypocrisy causes us."

The Presbyterian Church (U.S.A.) expends an incredible amount of energy "trying to conserve itself," David asserts. "By doing that, it maintains the white male traditional clergy as the mainline image and misses out on the beautiful plurality of God's wonderfully diverse creation. Look what happened with women and other minorities. As the church accepted women and ordained them, it pushed them to be as 'white male' as they can be. And look what happened when some tried to be creative and share some gifts women have to the ministry. A few years ago, various Protestant denominations supported a gathering of women called the 'Reimagining Conference.' Women from all over the world attended. They looked at images the Bible gives us for God. Many are not male images. The institutional church went zonkers! God help us should we continue to look for more wisdom from God and more revelations from the Bible! The church is creating a big sin by not looking at all of God's creation and seeing the gifts that each part of it has to offer."

Gay and lesbian ministers could, with the General Assembly's passage of less restrictive policies, bring many gifts to the church. "One of those gifts is to help the church break through its glass house regarding sexuality," David explains. "Heterosexual Christians do not feel comfortable with sexuality, for the most part. It is always mentioned as something to be controlled. But how often do we recognize it as part of the creation and thank God for it? Can you imagine someone thanking God for our sexuality in a community prayer? Yet, our sexual impulses are probably the strongest impulses we have. They are connected with our physical, emotional, and yes, our spiritual lives. I think gays and lesbians, because we've had to figure out our sexuality and learn to live creatively and responsibly with it, have this realization, among other things, to bring to the church. As Christians, we should always be open to God's showing us new things and thinking in new ways."

But a component of homosexuality that bothers many heterosexual Christians most, according to David, is the thought of sexual intimacy between two same-sex partners. The duplicity bred by the Presbyterian Church, as well as other Christian communities, can be partially attributed to the failure of church polity to deal with its own discomfort. "In the final analysis, what makes people sick is the actual thought of two men or two women having sex together," he says. "Part of the problem revolves around the fact that most human beings don't know how to live out their own sexuality. What do you do with all those feelings you have? Poor, straight men are taught that to be a man, you have to cough, spit, scratch your balls, and 'do it' in the missionary position. In my experience, only straight people who are very comfortable with themselves and their own sexuality are not afraid of rainbow people. They look at us as different, to be sure—but nothing to be afraid of. If we are not comfortable with our sexuality, we are afraid of anything 'different.' Minister types are often the worst. The most hateful, antigay preachers are precisely the ones caught in wild sex scandals at some point in their careers. I believe it is because they do not understand and appreciate this wonderful, mysterious part of creation. And I believe that rainbow people can help the church come to that understanding, that appreciation."

David offers a case in point. "I've experienced the most transcendental nature of God when I experience my spirituality with others," David explains. "Group prayer, and prayer with others, changes relationships among people. Good sex with my partner is more than just the two of us enjoying our physical sexuality. A third dimension exists in that physical exchange. I have always thought of it as being God, allowing us to speak to one another in a nonrational way, truly showing the love and care that God has given us. Indeed, it is often through having sex that we forgive one another in ways we couldn't have before."

Although David knows his denomination would "kick me out" if it discovered his sexual orientation, he intends to continue ministering as long as he can. "I need to stay in my denomination and help it change," he explains. "I have much respect for the MCC and may find the day comes when I can no longer be helpful in the struggle within my own denomination. Then, I will need to leave. But I also keep thinking of all those young rainbow people in my denomination who will one day face the same situation as I do now. If the day comes and I'm outed and removed from the ministry, I will need to decide what to do then. My hunch is that I'd stay in my denomination and fight from the lay angle."

David's idea of effecting change within the Presbyterian Church is patterned after Jesus' ministry. "Our leader was a Jew who criticized and tried to call his own religion to task for being too caught up in the rules and not loving each other," he explains. "They had missed the point and gotten off track. I don't think Jesus was trying to start a new religious institution. He was on the margins, speaking with and for those on the margins. To really please God, you have to love God, which means loving your neighbor. That's all the commandments wrapped up in one, according to the Christ. We need to listen to all people who are marginalized. Christ *is* the poor and the marginalized."

In Christ-like empathy with marginalized Christians, David sees a glimmer of hope. "Where would we be without straight supporters?" he asks. "They keep me sane. Sometimes, when I think about what I'm doing—living such a double life—I wonder if I'm nuts. But our best straight friends are those who are very comfortable with us. They include my partner and me in their family activities and treat us as any other couple. I think sympathetic straight clergy possibly have it worse than we do. How can they be supportive in this issue? Some of my straight friends have said that the day the church begins to fire rainbow people is the day they will lay their ordination down as well. That means a lot to me, because it says we are all in this together."

In fact, honest friendships with both homosexual and heterosexual ministers help David combat a threatening sense of alienation. "I relate candidly with other gay and lesbian ministers who have dealt with this issue in different ways," he says. "But often, gay and lesbian ministers are not really understood by the rainbow community. Many think that if you were really an activist, you would either leave the church or be in its face all the time. That's always been a problem. But I have another take on things. Although my sexual orientation [shapes who I am], I am also a person of faith. My commitment to ensuring that all God's people are loved and treated justly is also me. To put my cause ahead of anyone else's—well, that would be my issue. We need people to do that, of course—to focus on gay and lesbian issues exclusively. But I think we need both to happen simultaneously. We can't divide ourselves anymore. Some people in the Presbyterian Church have become very destructive over this issue. They get fed up, feel hopeless, and then begin to gripe. They become very pessimistic. This reaction is natural, I think, but also dangerous. It can infect others. Some of them need to think of moving on because they're getting eaten up. Perhaps the Metropolitan Community Church is the place for them—or another inclusive tradition. There they can heal themselves and begin to minister again."

Although the PC(USA) prohibits her pastoral service on the parish level, Janie Spahr has not felt compelled to move to the MCC. Instead, she heads up "That All May Freely Serve" (TAMFS), an organization of dedicated Presbyterians struggling within the denomination to enable gay, lesbian, bisexual, and transgender people to serve openly as clergy, elders, and deacons. The organization, a joint project of the Downtown United Presbyterian Church in Rochester, New York, and the Westminster Presbyterian Church in Tiburon, California, began in March of 1993 as a catalyst for change within the denomination. Education and dialog comprise the two vehicles through which activism occurs.[18] Originally, the efforts of TAMFS began with Janie's visits to faith communities, universities, college divinity schools, and private homes. Soon, teams traveled with her from the Downtown United

Presbyterian Church across the nation far and wide to share experiences directly attributable to homosexual orientation, or loving someone gay, lesbian, bisexual, or transgender. Through their stories, parents provide insights into the formative years of gay or lesbian youth, while gay and lesbian clergy put a face on ordination policies that restrict service to Christ despite their having met all ordination requirements—except those prohibiting a gay or lesbian minister from "practicing."

In her travels, Janie "puts a face" on the controversy—her own. "My former husband helped love me into myself," Janie recalls. "But I knew from the age of fourteen what I was supposed to do with my life—and that was to serve God as a Presbyterian minister."

At Pennsylvania State University, Janie not only studied world religions, but also explored a variety of faith communities, both Christian and non-Christian. Janie met Jim Spahr the summer before going to Penn State University. They became friends, began to date, and were married in 1964. "Jim is a wonderful guy who loved me, and who helped me love me," Janie says.

Shortly after their wedding, they moved back from California to Pittsburgh, the city where Janie was raised. "There, I met Wanda Graham Harris, an amazing African-American woman who helped me become a better minister," she relates. "She was an inspiring coach. She would say: 'Woman, when you pray, open your hands. And stop reading those notes when you preach.' She embodied what faith could really be." Wanda also helped Janie understand what living in poverty really means. "Because of her, I saw Pittsburgh in a way I would never have known. Before Wanda, I never knew poverty. Firsthand, I saw profoundly the terrible destruction caused by racism. Jim, my two sons, and I became immersed in that community. We loved the people there, and they loved us back."

Once the community fully accepted Janie, Wanda sent her a note: "Welcome to my world."

"But I worked in Hazelwood for only a short time," Janie says, sadly. "I was called to another ministry. Before I left, I told Wanda the truth—that I was a lesbian."

"Oh, I know, Janie," was Wanda's simple reply. "So what will you do for God?"

Janie followed her path from the inner city of Pittsburgh to a church in a wealthy suburban area near San Francisco. "The youth at First Presbyterian Church of San Rafael came to me about all kinds of things," she continues. "We dealt with alcoholism and incest, problems effectively camouflaged by this lovely area of California. But these youth told the truths of their lives. They did not hide what was happening in their lives. As they told me their stories, I was plunged into mine."

One afternoon, a nervous young man entered Janie's office. He seemed to be shaking all over. "I have to tell you something," he blurted out. "I have to tell you that I'm gay."

Janie moved next to him and placed an arm around his shoulders. "Me, too," she said.

"And there we were, hugging each other, acknowledging and celebrating the truth of who we are," Janie says.

Shortly before the young man's visit, the PC(USA) initiated a study of gay and lesbian issues within the denomination. In 1976, the majority report decreed that if a ministerial candidate is qualified, regardless of sexual orientation, the church should have the right to ordain him or her. However, in 1978, a less inclusive minority report overturned the ruling of the majority. Because Janie's ordination occurred before 1978, the Presbyterian Church could not revoke her credentials. However, the controversy, occasionally growing vitriolic and offensive, prodded Janie toward courage. "Jimmy, I want to say out loud who I really am," she told her husband. "I am a lesbian."

"I've been waiting for a year for you to tell me," Jimmy replied. "Now, let's go tell the boys."

Their two sons took Janie's news in stride. "Isn't this great?" one son said. "Let's tell the church."

Janie laughed. "I don't think the church is going to be nearly as thrilled as we are," she replied. "And since then, it has certainly proven so," she adds quietly.

In California, when the Oakland Council of Presbyterian Churches announced an opening, Janie accepted a position. However, word of Janie's sexual orientation spread through the ranks, producing some dissension.

"We love your work," a Council member assured her. "But you're a lesbian. We're afraid the council will dissolve if you stay."

To preserve an organization in whose value she believed, Janie resigned. "At precisely that moment, I was struck by the realization that I might not be able to do what I want with my life."

Next, Janie worked in a nursing home. "As I bathed these elderly people—some of them dying—and cleaned their rooms, I was gradually coming back to life," she continues. "I was ready to ask God the question, 'What will I do?'"

Meanwhile, Jim called the Metropolitan Community Church in San Francisco without Janie's knowledge, urging the church leadership to hear Janie preach. "I served MCCSF for two years, and had the most wonderful experience, this integration of being lesbian and Christian," she says. "We were in the heart of the Castro when AIDS began to hit. How I loved our people. This congregation set me free. There's nothing like a happy lesbian, gay, bisexual, or transgender Christian."

Following her service to MCCSF, Janie was called to direct the Ministry of Light, later named Spectrum, which began as a Presbyterian "ministry of reconciliation that provides services with God's gay and lesbian children."

Meanwhile, Jim had fallen in love with "a dear friend of mine." He asked Janie to officiate at their wedding ceremony. She joyfully agreed. "After the service, Jim reminded our sons that he and Jackie would have more respect and praise than I and my partner, Connie, would ever enjoy. Jim was just wonderful, as always. Our children were incredibly aware of gay, lesbian, bisexual, and transgender persons who attended their church. And because a number of Presbyterians were willing to 'person' the issues at General Assemblies and during other opportunities, this movement continues strongly today. Now, it has assumed a life of its own. But those were amazing years."

Then, in 1991, during a break between sessions at a church conference, "a childhood friend whom I hadn't seen in many years made a point to mention that her church was a More Light church that had an opening for a co-pastor. She promised to send me some information."

Within days, Janie received the material.

Months passed. Finally, Janie rediscovered the job description buried beneath a stack of books and papers on her desk. "I loved working with Spectrum," Janie explains. "We had many programs going well in the community. But after reading this job description of an opening at Downtown United Presbyterian Church, I grew pensive."

That night, she read the job description aloud to Connie. "It sounds like you," Connie said simply.

At four o'clock the following morning, Janie awoke. She kept hearing Connie's words, over and over again.

Change lurked on the horizon, but Janie wasn't quite ready to make a decision. "I spoke with people who had died from AIDS—people on the other side," she explains. "People I loved, and who invited me to be with them through their illness and untimely deaths. I knew they were speaking to me. When I hear that gays and lesbians have no spiritual value, I wish the people who feel that way would accompany [the staff of TAMFS] for just one day. Just come along and see that we are spiritual to our bones. During those years, when AIDS was bombarding our community mercilessly, I buried many close friends. They took me with them to the other side. At the same time, my years working at Spectrum gave me such clarity about the scapegoating that goes on against us. Yes, our country has a tremendous problem of heterosexism, sexism, and racism; added to this is a tremendous problem of classism and power-over situations, too. There is nothing spiritually or ethically right about this power-over privilege and naming situation. There is nothing equal about the dialog [about gay and lesbian issues] that occurs today in our churches. It is a power-over situation, and we [as gay and lesbian Christians] have no voice or vote. Instead, the churches continue to invite people to lie about our very being. They are complicit in our deaths, whether physical or spiritual. Because of the stance of so many churches, many of us have died from the inside out; many of us have died from spiritual suicide. So, keeping all these things in my mind, I examined this opportunity that had been placed before me. I called the chair of the search committee. It scared me for a moment to think I would even consider making this change. What if the church really might be interested even in an interview? But I knew I had to find out where they were in their search process. So many months had passed, and I thought they may have completed the process."

Janie was instructed to submit a personal information form to Downtown United Presbyterian Church. She met a pastor who had said to "let the church love you back." In her personal information form, she spoke of Connie, her partner, and compared God to her grandmother, the afghan-maker, who stitches each piece just a little bit differently—so full of color, so creative in her design. "This is a good mental exercise," she thought, "even if nothing else comes of it."

Then, the search committee requested an interview. Janie agreed. During the interview, the committee never once asked her about being lesbian. "For the first time since coming out in my experience with a Presbyterian church, no one made an issue of my sexual orientation," she explains. "Instead, the nominating committee asked me what work I had done to make me fit to fill this particular job description."

Janie pulled out of the co-chair's driveway where the meeting was held and began the first leg of her journey home. Suddenly, she pulled over and stopped the car. Through her tears, she looked at Connie. "There *are* people who take my work seriously," she said.

"It was such a beautiful experience for me," she whispers.

The committee called once again with good news. Janie was voted one of the final candidates. "Let me say I am deeply moved," she said when she met the committee again. "And there are questions I would like you to consider. If you have a gay or lesbian pastor, your secrets will come out. You know that, don't you? There will be lots of truthtelling."

But despite Janie's challenge, the parishioners at the church moved closer to her heart. "This experience was so moving and sacred to me," she explains. "John and his wife, Carolyn, parishioners there, had two small children. John told me something I'll never forget. 'You know what, Janie? It would be wonderful if you came here. It would be horrible if my children never got to know you.'"

Finally, Janie asked the committee to pray. "If you don't hear in prayer that I'm your final candidate, then please, don't ask me to come and serve with you," she said. "It would be very helpful to me, if you would pray first, and then let me know what you hear when you pray."

Several days later, each member of the search committee called to confirm that Janie was, indeed, their candidate of first choice. "Then I realized I needed to pray, to think about the offer," she says. "I've learned throughout the years that I have to hear deep inside. For the entire week, I was beside myself because I couldn't hear."

Finally, Dave Martin, the leader of Spectrum's AIDS work, brought a shirt into Janie's office, and draped it across her desk. The shirt had once belonged to Bob—a community leader Janie knew who died of AIDS. "You are out of your skin over this decision," Dave said. "I think you need your friends from the other side."

Still, Janie couldn't hear the call. She and Connie took a long, contemplative walk along the beach. Nothing. Then, she traveled to a local Presbyterian church she had attended years ago and sat on the steps leading to the sanctuary. "I saw a large black woman with her arms around Connie and me," Janie relates. "The woman was smiling. She arose and appeared in the aisle in a multicolored robed dress and a beautiful hat. I saw—*awesomeness.*"

"Didn't we do well with the Ministry of Light?" the woman asked, referring to Spectrum.

"Yes," Janie answered.

"Then trust me."

"But how do you tell about this kind of experience to a bunch of Presbyterians?" Janie laughs. "I remember that as I drove home, I could feel Her sitting beside me. I felt sadness, too—the sadness of God, who longs for us to be free. The last time, when I was speaking out on behalf of our community, I was doing it *for* God. Now, I felt I was being called to this ministry *with* God."

When she got home, she called the church to accept the position as one of four co-pastors. For two hours, the committee asked questions—questions to which Janie responded calmly and confidently. "I knew I had been called to the Downtown United Presbyterian Church," she says. "I knew we were to be in ministry together. I remember being so filled with the spirit. I also felt my friends' presence from the other side. There were so many angels in the room. These were moments I will never forget."

Other memorable—but less joyful—moments followed.

Within days, ten of the seventy-six member churches of the presbytery challenged Janie's call. "A stay-of-enforcement was issued that prohibited my service to Downtown United, but I was allowed to visit the Downtown Church," she recalls. "The entire year, we waited, confident that the General Assembly would vote in the affirmative. For so long, we had been waiting, thinking we were going to win. On the day Bill Clinton was first elected president, the General Assembly Permanent Judicial Committee overturned the Synod decision. I was told the call had been denied. Connie and I prayed for that wonderful congregation, but also for the people who voted no. And I thought: Did I give false hope to my gay and lesbian friends? Did I give false hope to my children, who were then grown men, saying to me: 'The church will do the right thing'? One son was present at the Synod trial. He heard his own mother equated with child molesters. It was one of those moments with your children. It was the only time during the trial that I cried. My son was furious."

In short order, the Downtown United Presbyterian Church began "to dream of calling me as an evangelist. The church's co-pastors named our mission project 'That All May Freely Serve.' Now Janie, they told me, go out and put a human face on this issue and spread the good news of God's love for all people. Since March 1993, my life has become this mission."

Tough, intolerant rhetoric threatens to undermine the good work that Presbyterians have already done. "When people are fearful, a more rigid theology comes into being," Janie explains. "So many Christians have a tremendous misunderstanding of who we are. Gay and lesbian Christians are willing to come forward, affirming our identities, affirming our lives, confirming our faith. After our speaking engagements, farmers have said: 'You're real; you're like the earth.' Once people meet us and hear our stories, their hearts and minds are opened, and many people come out to their congregations. Gays and lesbians are members of the families of folks who publicly describe us as the anti-Christ. Scapegoating makes people into the other—even family members. That's why we are still here, in this capacity. We are here to educate, inform, and advocate for an inclusive church where lesbian, gay, bisexual, and transgender people are welcome, where pertinent and relevant truths of our lives are honored and not legislated as immoral or deviant. We were *raised* by Christians in the very churches that condemn us, so come on! As Christians, we have no choice but to do justice. We *must* change structures. We *must* change systems of oppression and poverty and class. You betcha, being a Christian is about justice. It's about *doing* and *being* justice. It's the core of our faith."

In Janie's view, "the church didn't become upset with us until we got healthy—until we said we'd like to work beside you. Until we found our voices, we were seen as immoral, unfaithful, gone-awry people. When we claimed our voices, the church balked. Now, we have to say to the church: 'You are asking us to lie about our very being. You are inviting us to lie about ourselves.' I'm angry about a church that will *invite* its parishioners, their families, and clergy to lie."

Many Christians purport that homosexuality defies scriptural teachings. But if churches want to "get scriptural, then let's *really* get scriptural. If we want to learn what the Bible says, let's get down to what Jesus was really teaching. Christendom is long gone; it's time for Christianity to begin. Let's look closely at what that means. Christendom has to do with empires and kingdoms of glory. Christianity, however, changes kingdom to kin-dom. We need to return to our roots—and we can, when we answer one simple question with integrity. How do we treat the widow, the orphan, and the stranger? How are we doing? These exclusionary policies will be changed because it is the Christian thing to do."

Churches That Lie

The Evangelical Lutheran Church in America (ELCA) has periodically expressed its commitment to the quiet study of gay and lesbian issues as they affect its churches, but the witness of various Lutheran ministers reveals that, to the ELCA, commitment largely means issuing an annual pledge of hospitality for gay and lesbian worshipers. Meanwhile, gay and lesbian Lutheran ministers hear of their institution's "support" of the Employment Nondiscrimination Act (ENDA) and its official valuation of the gifts of homosexuals. However, they also understand that acknowledging a homosexual relationship could easily mean disaster because, like other mainline denominations, the ELCA provides pulpit access only to heterosexual clergy and to celibate gay and lesbian clergy. To come out means becoming immediately suspect.

In May 1996, the ELCA Division of Outreach pledged to enact "strategies to gay and lesbian people, especially in communities where there are large populations of homosexual persons, either with new ministers or through existing congregations."[19]

"Young men and women who are lesbian and gay are welcomed and affirmed by the bar crowd, by the sex crowd, and by the drug crowd," said Rev. Joseph E. McMahon, the Division of Outreach chair. "They are not welcomed by the church crowd, and we have to reverse that. We have to let these young people know that they are every part of God's creation as are all of us. We are their partners on this journey."

In March 1997, Lutheran Campus Ministry hosted a conference at the University of Michigan called "The Gifts We Offer, the Burdens We Bear: The Vocation and Ministry of Gay and Lesbian Persons in Church and Society." The conference intended "to provide an opportunity in which the gifts of gay and lesbian people among us could be celebrated, could be made visible, but also that the burdens they realistically face in our church could be faced," said the conference organizer, Rev. John Rollefson.

The conference centerpiece was a report, "Pulpit Fiction," which surveyed thirty-five gay and lesbian pastors to determine their degree of adherence to the ELCA policy which states that "practicing homosexual persons are precluded from the ordained ministry of this church." Of the thirty-five pastors, twenty-one reported involvement in committed, long-term relationships. "While our pastors were often anxious about coming out to other persons, they generally had no such problems with God," said Carolyn J. Riehl, project director and assistant professor of education at the University of Mexico. "These pastors want to be intimately connected to someone else, and they want that connection to be with a 'mutual, chaste, and faithful relationship,' as is the vision of the ELCA for its heterosexual ordained ministers."[20]

In her keynote address, Lutheran social ethicist and author Elizabeth Bettenhausen expressed a strong concern about ELCA policies toward its gay and lesbian clergy. "Whenever we as the church decide that a particular human characteristic is required in order to preach the gospel and administer the sacraments as means of grace, we have a theologically serious, weighty decision. . . . How do you engage in conversation when you have been church-defined in such a way that secrecy and silence are essential, if you want to stay in the pulpit?"[21]

On March 22, 1996, Bishops H. George Anderson and Charles H. Maahs released an "open letter" to member churches of the ELCA. "To gay and lesbian members," the letter began, "we write to you in hope and out of faith. We all live with the pain of a church that experiences sharp disagreements on some issues. Yet we walk beside you and we value your gifts and commitment to the Church. . . . [O]ur congregations should reflect on our Lord's invitation to all by being safe places for those who are persecuted or harassed in our society. We repudiate all words and acts of hatred toward gay and lesbian persons in our congregations and in our communities, and extend a caring welcome for gay and lesbian persons and their families."[22]

The bishops' "caring welcome" did not extend to ELCA clergy. During the same year, two San Francisco congregations were expelled from the ELCA for ordaining three homosexual persons not ELCA-approved because they refused to take the prerequisite vow of celibacy. The ordinations, which occurred in 1990, earned both churches five-year suspensions. When clergy Ruth Frost, Phyllis Zillhart, and Jeff Johnson still had their pulpits five years later, the ELCA Discipline Committee upheld the charges.

"Some people believe justice is being served in your being expelled," announced Robert Mattheis, bishop of the Sierra Pacific Synod, to the congregations. "But others regret the real tension and antagonism that was part of the process." St. Francis Lutheran Church and First United Lutheran Church were both removed from the ELCA roster.

"As far as they're concerned, I no longer exist," said Jeff Johnson, pastor of First United. "I perceived erroneously that the church was one of the greatest agents of social change. I still believe that to a point. But my goal is not institutional change because that will happen long, long, long after real change has taken place."[23]

In fact, "real change" had already begun at First United once the controversy arose. When the ELCA ordered the church to fire Johnson or be thrown out of membership, parishioners voted to risk expulsion. "He is who he is, and we love him for it," said May Vignola, seventy-five, a veteran member of forty-five years who stood behind "Pastor Jeff" all along.[24]

Other ELCA churches also began to follow their collective consciences.

In December 1997, St. James Lutheran Church in Kansas City, Missouri, adopted a "Statement of Intentional Welcoming." The statement says the church welcomes seekers who are not specifically Lutheran, persons of color whose primary language is not English, people of diverse economic backgrounds, traditional and single-parent families, people with physical, mental, and emotional disabilities—and gays and lesbians. Inclusion of the last group—gays and lesbians—stirred up a hornet's nest within the church.

"People argued genetics versus environment," said John Backus, pastor of St. James. "The argument is bogus because if we find out [homosexuality] is environmental, then we can teach people not to be gay. If we learn it's genetic, then in a few years we can correct it *in utero* or abort. We want to know this so we can fix it. But [homosexuals are] not broken. God didn't make them broken, whether through genetic or environmental [means]."

The following January, Backus received anonymous hate mail that missed the point entirely. "We're trying to be just," he said. "Our purpose is to do ministry with and among all the children of God who can find a home within these Lutheran doors. In our congregation, we believe that gay and lesbian people are not significantly different from our straight members. They are different as mechanics are different from accountants."[25]

Nor does St. James require celibacy from its homosexual members. "We say there should be faithful, loving relationships—committed relationships with no hitting and no cheating—the same as we expect of straight people," Backus explains. "Our word to their lives is the same. In this congregation, gay people are on boards. If you come to the altar to receive the Body of Christ, it is possible the hand that gives you the Body of Christ may be on gay or lesbian arms."

Mainline denominations could take twenty to fifty years to be fully accepting of homosexual parishioners, Backus predicts. "This is a justice issue," he says. "There are people within all church traditions who think it's a horrible thing to reach out to gays and lesbians. The question doesn't exist outside our faith. If we say the church has nothing to say to those who are gay and lesbian, that's obscene."

In many ELCA churches, the hands of a minister may belong to a gay or lesbian individual without the congregation's knowledge. The ELCA has done a thorough job of driving its ministers deeper into the closet. "If you're gay and are a 'practicing' gay person," says Keith Robinson, a Missouri minister of more than twenty years, "you can't be a Lutheran clergyperson under the present guidelines. Hence, one must choose between living the contradiction within an immoral church or 'coming out' and 'being out' of the church. I have been grappling with this issue since my seminary days in the early seventies when my ex-wife and I were part of Lutherans Concerned." In fact, Keith and his ex-wife helped with the inception and organization of this Lutheran support mechanism for gays, lesbians, and their allies. "You have to deal with it. If you come out, it's the end of your career."

Although Keith served as a parish pastor for six years, he has spent fifteen years in various specialized ministries sponsored by the ELCA, like participating in Latin American human rights initiatives. "But even when you're not in a pulpit Sunday after Sunday, it's difficult to be in social settings because of the pressures," he explains. "I've been partnered for six years. People like to come over to the pastor's house, so my partner and I have to be separated often. When people come over, he makes an excuse to leave."

The duplicity the closet breeds is "like wearing a mask—the kind of mask racial minorities must feel they're wearing," Keith says. "My partner is much more cautious than I. He is very aware that if [our partnership] becomes an issue, I will lose my job. So he's developed his own separate network of friends."

Despite the ELCA's repetitive call for dialog and reflection over homosexual issues, Keith is convinced that most Lutheran clergy support the present ordination policy. "Their vote would be no gays in the ministry," he says. "That's not to say that all clergy are unsupportive of gay and lesbian ministers. Some are quite angered by the hypocritical position of the Lutheran church: 'it's okay to be gay; just don't practice it.' By and large, the majority of ministers have fairly conservative attitudes. For lay people, homosexuality seems to be less of a problem. Until recently, I was out to very few straight Lutheran clergy."

Keith's HIV-positive diagnosis compelled him to come out to more individuals—particularly other Lutheran ministers. "That means taking a few risks to provide some support networks for myself, both personal and professional," he explains. "If something were to happen—if I should get sick—there needs to be a safety net. I would need help to sustain any project to which I have been called."

Yet, in building his support network, Keith has been shocked by the "lack of skills" among Lutheran clergy in relating to HIV-positive people. Once, when Keith returned to his office from a doctor's appointment, he told a friend that his T-cell count had decreased considerably.

"Oh, that's great!" the minister said.

"This guy thought a low T-cell count was a good thing," Keith continues. "There's a tremendous need among Lutheran clergy for AIDS education. I wonder how ineffective they would be to spiritually counsel someone who comes to them with the HIV virus or with AIDS."

Keith's view of human sexuality provides him with a conscious way to deal with and accept his sexual orientation. "Human sexuality is key to the intimacy and closeness that reflect the love and community that can exist between human beings," he explains. "That's part of what is life—and God-given in terms of being able to experience the sexuality of people—and I mean that in a very broad way. Lots of hugs, touches, and so forth, encourage people to be their best. We are created in God's image, and that includes gay and heterosexual people. The ability to express oneself selflessly and sexually to the person you're in love with is all God-given."

Lutheran belief statements do not specifically label homosexuality as a sin; human beings find affirmation in the fact of their creation.[26] However, a theological difficulty lies in the Lutheran prohibition against sexual intimacy with a committed other. "This internalized homophobia of the church is the sin," says Keith. "The strong, negative messages from the church—those are sins. The fact that I'm in a relationship does not mean I'm committing a sin. Young people from fundamentalist and Baptist traditions find having that 'sin' [of being homosexual] is difficult to live with, but we need to unpack that baggage and live and celebrate. That's a slow process. If you think homosexuality is a sin, then you take less care of yourself and do risky things. You encounter obstacles toward establishing solid relationships. You might become more promiscuous and live more on the edge and become less affirming of self and others."

What closeted gay and lesbian Lutheran ministers have to realize, says Keith, is that "the church is a liar. We aren't. As it stands now, in my position, the burden of proof is on the bishop or the church to prove I'm gay. That's my own feeling. Sometimes, that's very hard to deal with, this idea of lying. There are times I have to discipline myself, just as every other gay and lesbian Christian does. What kind of relationship are we going to have with God? How do we understand the truth; how do we put this together? How do we find community? How can we receive a sacrament that is not reconciling in Christ? How do we accept sacraments from a pastor whose T-cell count is decreasing? The questions take you beyond the powers of this world, like becoming a medieval mystic. You have different eyes to see things because of who you are. Gays and lesbians have to be much stronger people in terms of insight and creativity. The people who make it through this struggle are not abashed; they tend to do much better spiritually."

Being stronger, in Keith's view, does not necessarily mean coming out. "I think, at this point in history, for a Lutheran clergy to say he or she is a 'practicing' gay or lesbian would be a dreadful mistake," he says. "It is ecclesiastical suicide. We don't live in an age when we need more martyrs. When that happens, how much is lost in the long-term? How much more has been lost, than gained?"

As this chapter earlier alluded, Steven P. Sabin, pastor of the Lord of Life Lutheran Church in Ames, Iowa, came out to his bishop in January 1997. During a tense conversation, Philip L. Hougen, the ELCA bishop of the Southeastern Iowa Synod, asked Steve directly if he was involved in a homosexual relationship with his partner, Karl Von Uhl. Rather than lie, Steve, the father of two daughters by a ten-year heterosexual marriage, admitted that he and Karl had been partners for five years. Consequently, the bishop asked Steve to resign. Steve refused.

"In May 1997, Bishop Hougen convened a consultation committee that met with Karl and me for four hours," Steve relates. "The committee actually recommended that the bishop not take any steps, because the issue was one of great controversy in church policy, and in church teaching, which required study and discussion. However, the bishop decided not to take the committee's advice."

Months later, in November 1997, after much "consideration, discussion and study," Bishop Hougen filed charges against Steve for engaging in "and continuing to engage in a pattern of conduct incompatible with the character of the ministerial office in that Pastor Sabin has persisted for more than five years in an active homosexual relationship with a male partner." The bishop requested the disciplinary action of "removal from the ordained ministry of this church."

However, Steve had already served as Lord of Life's pastor since 1985. Not only had the congregation seen Steve through his divorce in 1990; they had also met Karl.

Nevertheless, in early 1998, a disciplinary hearing was scheduled at a hotel conference room in downtown Des Moines.

"I was not included in the hearing," Karl relates. "Technically, two witnesses could be allowed inside. The hearing was closed, although the rules state that the accused can have two people to sit as counsel. I was to attend under that rubric—as counsel. But when I walked toward the meeting room, there was a fellow at the door who said, 'That man is not allowed in.' He was pointing at me."

During the hearing, Bishop Hougen stipulated that scriptural arguments could not be part of the debate. His reason? The nine-member church panel chosen to hear the case was not called to change church policy, but to determine whether it had been violated. "I understand why people want to make a public issue of this, and I think it's an important issue," Bishop Hougen said to the *Des Moines Register* (January 31, 1998). "My request to the hearing officer was to limit the discussion to the question of whether or not Pastor Sabin was living in conflict with church policy, and that we not get into theological arguments about whether or not the church has the correct position." Hougen added that he was "caught between the church's traditional teachings and a sense of compassion for people who feel very excluded or very hurt or denigrated by the church policy."

But Lord of Life church council member Marty Kelly estimated that 90 percent of the church's parishioners supported their pastor and encouraged him in his fight. "Almost everyone supported Steve," he told the *Des Moines Register* (February 2, 1998). "It definitely didn't fracture the congregation. Even the few people who left, I think, are still supportive of Steve as a person. We're looking at the man and what he does and can do. It's not the man, per se, but the way he preaches the word of the Lord."

Steve says only one family left the congregation, and that defection stemmed from publicity the charges had brought to the church.

"My personal feeling is that even if they de-roster Steve, we will ask him to stay as our pastor," added Kelly. "[We have] a family. We won't ask him to leave."

At the end of the two-day hearing, the panel reached its verdict. Steve would be removed from the active roster of Lutheran ministers, and Lord of Life would be asked to find another pastor. The panel admired the job Steve had done as pastor but could not allow his "gifts of ministry either to out-weigh or excuse" his violation of a church policy that bars "practicing homosexuals" from ordained ministry.

In short order, Steve and his lawyer decided to appeal "on the basis of denial of due process," Steve explains. "The verdict is unsupported by the record. The policy was improperly promulgated. Yet the results are even more inconsistent than that. Gay and lesbian people are welcome to fully participate in the life of the church, provided they are lay persons in the pew. 'Practicing' homosexuals are precluded from the ordained ministry and rostered lay positions. The church tends not to explain that policy at all. One thing the ELCA has been trying to write for ten years is a teaching statement. The ELCA has no official teaching on human sexuality. So, we are left with an un-Lutheran position that what is sinful for the clergy is not sinful for the laity. That's a tricky position because it defies the concept of the 'priesthood of all believers.' It makes clergy and rostered laity a different breed than the rest of the people in the congregations."

"The ELCA tends to view homosexuality as an orientation and as a behavior," adds Karl, his partner. "Invariably, one understanding negates the other."

"The implicit understanding of the church is that only homosexuals can resort to homosexual behavior," Steve explains. "As a joke, I asked if homosexual behavior is okay if it occurs between two straight men. The panel was not amused and did not respond. I pushed the issue to indicate how badly conceived in terms of human sexuality and church doctrine the policy is. The policy deals only with homosexual persons whose self-understanding is homosexual; *they* are to refrain from homosexual relationships. If I were straight, would a homosexual relationship really be okay?"

Nancy Lewis, a charter member of the twenty-five-year-old congregation, suspected Steve was gay shortly after his divorce. (Steve and his ex-wife have joint custody of their teenage daughters and are always "respectful and honest with each other.") When Karl came to town, she began to worry that Steve's homosexuality would upset others in the church. "On the other hand, he needed Karl," she said. "I believe God sent us Karl. Steve became warmer toward us and more open toward us. He had Karl to take care of him."

Steve and Karl "met" one another on the Internet—a "nineties romance," as Steve likes to call it. "Just like Rush Limbaugh met his third wife," interjects Karl, laughing. Then, more seriously, he adds: "I knew from the start Steve was clergy. And I respected that. Once this controversy began, the ELCA, in effect, denied me my humanity. I was no longer Steve's loving spouse, but a mere occasion to sin. It hurt more than I can describe to have the church personally attack me, invade my privacy—through my spouse, no less—and deny me any voice in the proceedings."

Steve came out to his entire congregation only when Bishop Hougen filed charges. "I made the announcement after the bishop asked for my resignation," he says. "I told people what many of them already knew, and still others suspected. An issue had arisen, I said, because the bishop asked for my resignation. I'm gay, I told them, and Karl is my partner. Before, a few people had asked: 'Karl? What's up with him?' I'd tell them the truth. Everyone has been supportive, although there were a number of tears that day. Some came up and told me how proud they were of me and how they appreciated being able to talk about sexual orientation issues more openly. Then they invited us to their house for dinner. Fortunately, the story didn't become an issue in the press for six months. By then, my congregation had time to assimilate the details. They were ready for the publicity."

The controversy also attracted new members to Lord of Life. "And yes, more gay and lesbian members have joined the church, and some veteran members have volunteered the information that they are gay or lesbian," Steve confides. "There was some concern about becoming a 'gay church,' but that's not something to worry about in Ames. We're a university town, and our homosexual folks are just like everybody else in the congregation."

Additionally, since 1993, Lord of Life has been a Reconciled in Christ congregation. "I had nothing to do with that, actually," explains Steve. "The proposal was put together by Catechism students. They had read about the gay-inclusive status and said, 'Gee, this is really great. Can we do that?' I said, 'Okay, fine. Here's the paperwork.' The congregation passed it without a hitch."

On September 28, 1998, Steve lost his appeal. His name was removed from the active roster of ELCA ministers. At that time, his congregation had not decided what to do. "If my congregation wants to keep me as their pastor, the ELCA can't do very much," Steve says. "They don't own the property. They could censure or expel my congregation from the ELCA. But I sense my parishioners don't want to lose me as their pastor, even though Bishop Hougen, at a recent congregational meeting, went on at great length stating that the synod *might* be able to help out with funding a new sanctuary if the church honors the ELCA's request."

"Apparently, bribery works in the service of the gospel," Karl quipped.

Defrocking by the ELCA was extremely painful for Steve. "I grew up in the Lutheran Church," he explains. "Because of my father's professional circumstances, my family moved around a lot. We lived in about twenty places during my childhood, and the Lutheran Church always provided a sense of stability in my life. Regardless of where my family lived, we knew the liturgy would be familiar; we had the same spiritual take on things. The local church would be a place to put down roots. I developed a sense of attachment, loyalty, and ownership." Steve pauses. "I'm a stubborn German. I think the bishop's wrong, and in my office I'm called to proclaim the truth in season and out of season."

Why were Steve's parishioners able to handle the controversy so well? "First of all, the congregation has a strong tradition of being a diverse group," Steve explains. "We invite people who are often alienated to become members of our church. We have a racially diverse mix, including several interracial couples. We have people who have been in trouble with the law, and who have gone through messy divorces. Of course, I'd like to think they responded well because the congregation struggles and strives to be first and foremost in the expression of the body of Christ. They are not about everybody being the same thing, nor are they from a uniform political perspective. They are about proclaiming the gospel. They are able to proceed from the perspective that God accepts people regardless of their race or sexual orientation. Admittedly, too, I've had a long-time pastorate with them. They went through my divorce with me. We've had time to build a relationship and trust."

Steve feels that church traditions should acknowledge an often ignored reason for allowing gay and lesbian clergy to serve openly. "We wouldn't suggest that one minister equipped for urban ministry should be placed in the Plains, would we?" he asks. "The needs of Lord of Life may not be precisely the needs of another church. The irony of the ecclesiastical 'don't-ask-don't-tell' policy is that it increases the likelihood that a congregation may get a gay pastor, whether they want one or not."

Regardless of the congregation's response—or Steve's—Karl says his partner's "call to minister and his relationship with God are very palpable and very profound. There's nothing that will sever that, not even this."[27]

Although gay and lesbian ministers remaining in mainline faith communities work in a variety of ways for inclusion and justice, others have severed their ties with denominations whose practices vacillate from year to year or from situation to situation. They have found their relationship with God demeaned and disparaged, often in the same denominations that nurtured them into adulthood.

When pastoral gifts are valued only within church documents issued once a year, many gay and lesbian ministers are left with few options. Some choose to leave their faith communities for denominations like the Unitarian Universalist Association, the United Church of Christ, or the Metropolitan Community Church. In these denominations, their expanding talents are celebrated. They preach as visionaries in a new land where their lives and their loves are cherished, respected, and affirmed.

4

VISIONARIES IN A NEW LAND

Honest, Healthy Lives

While most faith communities struggle to establish "acceptable" parameters of gay and lesbian affirmation and inclusion, yet balk at the prospect of ordaining "practicing homosexuals," three visionary denominations—the Unitarian Universalist Association, the United Church of Christ, and the Universal Fellowship of Metropolitan Community Churches—have taken significant strides toward establishing a heightened comfort level among heterosexual parishioners who worship among gay men and lesbians. Rather than thwarting the dialog of inclusion with literal scriptural interpretation, professionally discounted psychological theories advocating the homosexual person's need or capacity for change, or stereotypical generalizations about gay and lesbian lives, these three faith communities regard Christianity's true message as one of spiritual liberation—a liberation that cannot occur without full, honest acknowledgment of one's identity. Visionary churches do not regard homosexuality as a stumbling block to full fellowship. In fact, they accept homosexuality as proof of God's diverse creation, equal to but no better (or worse) than heterosexuality. Gay and lesbian parishioners and clergy are extended acceptance befitting such respectful regard.

Most mainline denominations continue to lose parishioners because their churches seem anachronistic in a dynamically changing world. But the Unitarian Universalist Association (UUA) continues to experience increasing membership. Noncreedal in nature—in other words, although its historical roots can be traced to Jewish and Christian traditions, UUA considers itself neither—Unitarian Universalism is a liberal religion that "keeps an open mind to the religious questions people have struggled with in all times and places."[1] According to the denomination's guiding principles, religious authority is not inherent in a book or institution, but can be found through personal experience, conscience, and reason. The UUA has provided, for many, answers to the questions that plague them as "Christians in exile"—a term Episcopal Bishop John Shelby Spong uses to characterize those people of faith for whom Christianity as it is largely practiced and preached today fails to answer their spiritual needs.[2]

For biblical "literalists," the UUA would be an uncomfortable fit. For those who perceive the quest for spiritual growth as fluid, dynamic, and adventurous, the principles of the UUA are indeed enticing. Over one thousand congregations throughout the United States encourage the "principled search for truth while practicing justice, equity, and compassion in human relations."[3] A familiar theological principle to Christians is Jesus' commandment to respond to God's grace by loving their neighbors selflessly—a commandment that Unitarian Universalists acknowledge as their philosophical bridge to Christian communities. That call to selfless love extends to gay and lesbian laity and clergy in the UUA; in fact, for more than twenty-five years, the denomination, headquartered in Boston, has had an Office of Bisexual, Gay, Lesbian, and Transgender Concerns.

Keith Kron, the Office's director, was raised a Southern Baptist but has been a Unitarian Universalist for over thirteen years. "The Southern Baptist Convention's stance on homosexuality had everything to do with my joining the UUA," Keith says. "While I was a high school senior, my Sunday School class was discussing homosexuality. One of my teachers looked directly at me."

"Don't get me started," she said sarcastically. "Homosexuals are sick people. Isn't that right, Keith?"

Such an attitude would never be expressed by the UUA, whose General Assemblies have issued a number of positive policy statements about homosexual rights. In 1970, the UUA called for an end to discrimination against homosexuals and bisexuals, followed by the 1973 establishment of the Office Keith now directs. In 1980, the UUA actively began to assist in assigning gay and lesbian ministers to specific churches. In 1984, it supported ministers in performing same-sex services of union. Since then, other actions have included refusal of the UUA to conduct business with companies that discriminate against gays and lesbians, support of the legalization of same-sex marriage, and inclusion of transgender people in the life of the Unitarian Universalist Church.

Experiencing the acceptance of the Unitarian Universalist tradition changed Keith's perception of his own sexual orientation. "Before UUA, I saw being gay or lesbian as being a fragment of one's life," he explains. "Now I see it as being a more integrated part. It's more of a woven fabric as opposed to strips laid side by side."

Furthermore, leaving the Southern Baptist tradition compelled Keith to analyze his relationship with Christianity. "I view myself as a christian with a small 'c,'" he says. "God has significant meaning for me in my life. Jesus has an even closer meaning, in some ways, than he does for Pentecostals. I would not, however, identify myself as being trinitarian."

Keith fills an important role by working with congregations who have petitioned for a "Welcoming" status—a simple designation for churches ready to open their doors to full fellowship with gays and lesbians. Presently, almost

20 percent of all UUA congregations have earned the designation, in effect since 1987, when the UUA's Common Vision Planning Committee discovered many negative attitudes, deep prejudices, and profound ignorance about gay men and lesbians. As a result, the UUA developed a series of workshops for churches wanting to make gay and lesbian worshipers feel at home. A "Welcoming Congregation" insists on inclusive language and content in its worship, while fully incorporating the experiences of gay, lesbian, bisexual, and/or transgender people throughout all church programs. It also reaches out to the gay and lesbian community in its advertising and by actively supporting gay and lesbian groups. The Welcoming Congregation celebrates the lives of all people, including same-sex couples, recognizing their committed relationships and equally affirming displays of caring and affection. Congregations go through ten to fourteen workshops before they earn the designation.

"Being accepted in a congregation is a primary concern among gay and lesbian parishioners," Keith explains. "Acceptance operates on many different levels. Some folks will say it's okay for gays and lesbians to worship with them. But when partners, sitting in the pews among other parishioners, put their arms around each other, that simple gesture of affection might catch some members of the congregation off-guard. We encourage congregations to ask themselves a number of questions and to answer them honestly. What does it mean for gays and lesbians to have the same privileges that heterosexual couples do? What exactly is appropriate behavior? Sometimes, I hear members express fear that if they become Welcoming, their congregation might become a gay church. But what would be wrong if the church became primarily gay? Would heterosexuals not feel welcomed there? Is that concern not illustrative of work that remains to be done? However, it's very unlikely that the church would become exclusively gay. That simply *never* happens."

Although ordination in the UUA is open to both homosexual and heterosexual clergy, Keith's office still faces challenges in finding suitable congregations for gay and lesbian ministers. "Here's where I think we are," he explains. "If you are openly gay or lesbian, you still have to be an exceptional minister to be placed. Even an *average* straight minister can be placed fairly easily. So, something of a double standard still exists in the UUA. However, on the upside, we have one lesbian couple who serve as co-ministers in one congregation."

As an ordained UUA minister, Keith's view of the current arguments in Christian traditions over homosexual ordination and affirmation boils down to "conversations that Unitarian Universalists hate having. Still, it's one we really need to start engaging in. But we haven't been willing to talk to people of other religious traditions—particularly fundamentalists." In 1997, Keith served on an interfaith panel in Nashville, Tennessee, on "Gender, Religion, and Sexuality." "All kinds of folks were in attendance," he says. "The guy next to me introduced himself as being to the right of the Right. He laughed when I introduced myself as being left of the Left. I had an easier time talking to conservatives than the people in the middle. We agreed on what we believed and were able to express our belief differences with clarity. I sensed more respect [from the fundamentalists] than from Episcopalians and Lutherans. The Religious Right values clarity, which, unfortunately, takes the form of rigidity. Still, we looked honestly at how we would get along since we don't agree. It's useful to experience both sides of this conversation. What I discovered is that mainline churches often say nothing. In essence, those are the churches who send out mixed messages. People wonder what they really believe." Even so, Keith wonders how fundamentalists can possibly feel "at peace with God. I get really concerned about theology that says God loves you only if you're a particular way."

"Reverend Anna" was an ordained minister in a mainline Protestant tradition for fifteen years before she defected to the UUA in 1995. She uses a pseudonym to protect her children, for she is unwilling to enlist them involuntarily in her battles. "I consider myself an ethical Christian," she explains. "I follow the ethics of Christ, but I don't believe in his divinity."

When Anna was seventeen years old, she decided to pursue her call to the ministry. "I was in love with God, and I wanted to work in the church," she says. But her theology shifted, and the tradition in which she was originally ordained grew less and less comfortable. Finally, she realized she had to make a change. "When I was assigned as interim minister at the Unitarian Universalist church in Spartanburg (South Carolina), I came out to the board."

"I've struggled with this for four years," she said to the board members. "I want to live my life with integrity. To do that, I need to live my life as a lesbian."

For a moment, the room was silent. "I'm not sure how to put this information in the minutes," the board secretary finally said.

"Put it like this," the board president replied. "We went into executive session, and then we came out."

"I told them I did not intend to deal with my homosexuality from the pulpit," Anna continues. "I got the impression they really didn't care one way or the other. They were just relieved I wasn't quitting."

Despite the level of tolerance among her parishioners, her church has not earned a Welcoming Congregation designation. The congregation began the process before Anna came aboard, but the process went awry. "Some very strident members of the gay and lesbian community were less than tactful," she explains, "as were some very outspoken straight members. They were polarized by bad manners and name calling. The conflict got really personal."

For example, a straight parishioner once expressed the concern that the church might become known throughout the community as "that gay church." "That's the most homophobic thing I've ever heard," another straight member retorted, creating a profuse defensiveness among parishioners of both sexual orientations.

Because of the vitriol, the church lost members. "For now, the process has been set aside," Anna continues. "Besides, I feel like we're already a welcoming congregation."

The assertion that the combination of the love of Christ and faithful prayer can change gays and lesbians into heterosexuals strikes Anna as misguided. "Sure, you could kill that thing inside you," she says. "You could suffocate it. You could go around with it rattling in your chest. I don't believe that [ex-gay] movement can transform anyone into a fully alive person. You become someone keeping her foot on the neck of her sexuality. You have to fill that emptiness with something else. Perhaps you could get a really good religious addiction going. But you won't find happiness."

As one might expect of a minister living in the Bible Belt, Anna is no stranger to fundamentalist rhetoric. Nor is she sheepish about debating Christians from that tradition. "That's one of my great joys," she says, laughing. "I've debated in letters to the editor. My character has been assassinated in the newspaper. I was even thrown off a radio broadcast once. It occurred during a talk show that I was hosting. In Spartanburg County, an antigay resolution was in the works." The resolution, which was ultimately passed by county council, proclaimed homosexuality discordant with community standards. In fact, the resolution caused several national businesses to withdraw plans for development in Spartanburg County. As a result of the potential economic backlash, the resolution was rescinded. "I arranged to interview two 'married' lesbians about their relationship," she continues. "I encouraged them to talk about their commitment. The broadcast originated in a local coffee shop. After fifteen minutes on the air, we broke for a commercial. During the commercial, the station owner called the coffee shop. He told me to get off the air because my content wasn't appropriate for a family radio station. He played music for the rest of the show."

According to Anna, who is originally from the Northeast, the local letters to the editor column provides a forum for every undereducated person in the area. "Such ignorant things appear frequently in the paper here," Anna says. "Recently, letter writers stated over and over that God is absolutely direct in designating homosexuality as an abomination. The letters poured in. Well, this time I refused to take the letter writers on. But I *did* question the paper's editorial judgment. In my own letter to the editor, I asked if the paper would print the undereducated rantings of a bigot that blacks and whites should not intermarry. Of course, that kind of letter would not appear, I asserted. Obviously, *someone* on the editorial staff is using some kind of judgment." Anna laughs. "What happened then? People wrote in to accuse me of being a horrible intellectual snob."

Anna is tired of "getting crumbs from the Bible's table. I'm tired of searching the Bible for elements of feminism or inclusiveness of sexual orientation so that I can have ammunition against the fundamentalists. In religion, our option—the option I'm most supportive of—is to broaden the base of spiritual authority past the Bible. But, unfortunately, for many people, the Bible is their only faith statement. I have deep sympathy for people who continue to wrestle with the Bible on the issue of homosexuality. It's a losing battle."

Bill Z. grew up as a Roman Catholic but switched to the Unitarian Universalist tradition because of his comfort with the idea "that I could have a theological belief in a broadly defined God that's not the old man in the sky, or a personal entity," he explains. "I wanted to be rid of all the baggage of trying to make sense of the Trinity. I could not have remained in the Catholic faith, even if Catholicism's stance on homosexuality were different."

For three years, Bill has served a Unitarian Universalist church in Austin, Texas. At first, his homosexuality alienated a small percentage of his congregation. Out of four hundred fifty members, about a dozen parishioners left when they learned a gay minister had been called to the church. "Now, when I interview or meet new members, I let them know about me right away," Bill says. "Usually, it doesn't matter at all. Sometimes, the fact that I'm gay is the reason they decided to join the church."

When he left his first church, Bill received two unique thank-you notes from elderly gentlemen. "From the start, they were apprehensive about having a gay man as a minister," Bill relates. "Now, they were thanking me for being who I am and for helping them to understand homosexuality a little more. They thanked me for helping them become comfortable with the idea of homosexuality, and with gay men. They thought my openness about my sexual orientation was my greatest gift to the congregation."

Rev. Meg Riley preceded Keith Kron as director of the Office of Bisexual, Gay, Lesbian, and Transgender Concerns. She also served as a parish educator in a UUA church in Minnesota. Now, she directs the Washington, D.C., Office for Social Justice. In the ongoing religious debate over homosexual issues, Meg feels, the mainline denominations are trying to fend off the fundamentalists. "A basic Universalist belief is that Jesus was a child of God, but so is each of us," Meg says. "We are embodied spirits. Jesus lived an exemplary life; so can we. We are all God's incarnations; our bodies, sexuality, and the earth are God's gifts. A sexual relationship—in my case, a homosexual one—is the way I'm connected to the world. It's one of the primary ways that I experience God's love. My partner and I have been together eight years. We have one child—a daughter. My family is one of the happiest realities of my life. My partner and I made the decision to be together—and to have a family together—with a great deal of support from our religious community. The UUA even pays for my partner's health care. It's a very nonhomophobic work environment. When I was a religious educator, however, I had two lives. It's great to be able to acknowledge my homosexuality and not be 'that lesbian minister.' I don't want to be held back by labels from reaching out across barriers [that separate people]."

Many gay and lesbian ministers in Christian traditions defect to the UUA—not to acclaim their homosexuality, not to make a political statement, but to worship and lead in a religious tradition where they are regarded as pastors, not objects of controversy. "It's a hard thing for them," Meg explains. "But there is a point where it's just self-abuse to stay in a hostile environment. No one who is outside the clergy can understand. So many circumstances within faith communities can be demeaning—like never acknowledging your partner. It's like ripping your arm off when you decide to leave one tradition and go to another. It's that hard, no matter how necessary. We ministers have a tendency to give ourselves away too much. When we're queer, we feel as though we can handle it."

One problem not easy to handle, however, is the ex-gay portrayal of homosexual lives as lost lives. Along with Urvashi Vaid, Director of the Policy Institute of the National Gay and Lesbian Task Force, and Jean Hardisty, Executive Director of the Political Research Associates, Meg, as the co-chair of the Steering Committee of Equal Partners in Faith, has officially denounced the ex-gay movement as "promoting an agenda for all Americans that is profoundly antidemocratic and exclusionary. . . . The ex-gay movement and the Christian Right are attacking these principles [of tolerance and pluralism] and furthering a divisive political agenda that offers fundamentalist Christian dogma and heterosexuality as the only acceptable norms. Challenging the leadership of the ex-gay movement is essential if equal rights for all people, regardless of sexual orientation, are to be defended." Furthermore, the ex-gay leadership's contention that hating the sin does not equate to hating the sinner doesn't work for Meg. "That's nothing short of gay bashing," Meg says. "Besides, it's a disturbance, this obsession with sexuality. It's a disturbance, this obsession with Bill Clinton's sex life. I think anybody who is obsessed with somebody's sex life is disturbed."

From the perspective of these clergy, demand by fundamentalists, whether in full-page newspaper ads, on protest signs, or from their pulpits, that gays and lesbians must retreat into their closets or "convert" to heterosexuality is a demand for dishonesty. "The God of the fundamentalists—well, that's a different God from the God that I know," Meg says quietly. "The healthier our lives are, the more honest we will become. The more honest we are, the more we will have a right relationship with God."

Although the Unitarian Universalist Association has moved closest to the full acceptance of gays and lesbians in its churches—including unconditional acceptance of holy unions between same-sex partners—many mainline Christians would tactfully discount theological justifications for such acceptance from a denomination that does not require commitment to a Christian theology. However, because UUA clergy openly explore spiritual questions from a variety of theological perspectives, their insights may help pave the way toward an honest appeal for answers. Over time, the UUA may establish an atmosphere of neutrality for the exploration of ways for faith communities to address issues of sexual orientation and spirituality. Integrity, curiosity, and compassion are surely values all people of faith can agree on.

To Seek a Balanced Faith

The United Church of Christ (UCC) has ordained openly gay and lesbian ministers—even those who are partnered—since 1972, when William R. Johnson became the first openly gay person to be ordained in any mainline denomination. In 1994, the University Congregational Church in Seattle, by a three-fourths majority, voted to call Peter Ilgenfritz and his partner, David Shull, as associate pastors. By 1996, three predominantly lesbian and gay congregations were numbered among the UCC flock in Cleveland, Minneapolis, and Kalamazoo.

Not that the UCC is without blemish in ministering to the spiritual needs of gays and lesbians, and in offering opportunities for service to its gay and lesbian clergy. Since 1985, UCC congregations have been free to apply for the status of "Open and Affirming (ONA)." Out of sixty-five hundred congregations, only three hundred have achieved that designation, despite the fact that, during 1985, the General Synod encouraged all UCC congregations to "study homosexuality" toward a future declaration of ONA status. Despite the denomination's affirming policies of ordination, gay and lesbian ministers find quickly that UCC ordination does not automatically ensure assignment to a congregation.

Neither has the United Church of Christ's openness to diversity been without controversy. In December 1997, a conservative religious group distributed fliers in several Milwaukee neighborhoods, condemning Stephen Welch, senior pastor of a UCC congregation, for his signature on a document declaring his support for an end to barriers against gays and lesbians in the religious community (*Milwaukee Journal-Sentinel,* December 16, 1997). "Pastor Welch does not believe that homosexual acts are sinful and, in fact, believes that it is wrong to be against homosexuality," the fliers stated.

But to his face, Welch received only positive feedback. "The general tenor—at least of what I hear—is anger and disgust at this kind of ploy," he said in his comments to the *Milwaukee Journal-Sentinel.* "I've heard from several [individuals] in the community—not only my own church family— who are supportive of my taking the affirmation that I did."

Welch's actions match both the spirit and the letter of the UCC's founding principles. When the denomination was formed in 1957, the three faith communities that merged into the UCC shared a strong commitment to the freedom of religious expression; in essence, the denomination was more concerned with what unites Christians rather than with issues and ideas that divide them. "The United Church of Christ embraces a theological heritage that affirms the Bible as the authoritative witness to the Word of God, the creeds of the ecumenical councils, and the confessions of the Reformation," the church's statement of beliefs asserts. "The UCC has roots in the 'covenantal' tradition—meaning there is no centralized authority or hierarchy that can impose any doctrine or form of worship on its members. Christ alone is head of the church. We seek a balance between freedom of conscience and accountability of the apostolic faith."

Nowhere is that commitment to balance more apparent than in the UCC's dialog about same-sex unions. Whereas most denominations still debate gay and lesbian ordination and inclusion, UCC has moved into a larger, more controversial, and more political arena.[4] Max L. Stackhouse, professor of Christian ethics at Princeton Theological Seminary, emphasizes a return to the "normative" structure of relationships, as divinely perceived during creation. That normative structure includes generativity. "The capacity to reproduce is a gift," he writes. "Generativity is a mark of how God invites creatures to participate in the blessing of ongoing creativity. This means, among other things, that humans are to see their sex as a part of the ongoing flow of life, as a blessed link in the generations, becoming fathers and mothers to the generations of tomorrow in a way that can be honored." Stackhouse concedes that God may recognize even greater moral integrity in some nonsexual same-sexed affections than in heterosexual marriages. In other words, two men or two women may love one another—as long as that love is not expressed carnally—in a wholesome, honest way that rivals the best of relationships between men and women. "Nevertheless, these affections are not something that can and should displace the common expectation that we should . . . approximate the primary structures and purposes of human sexuality given in creation." He believes strongly that Christians should be tolerant of sexual diversity, "especially legally, but we should not engage in or approve behavior that increases the likelihood of abortion or war, even if some people genuinely feel desires that could lead to those results. Similarly with homosexuality."

Although Stackhouse does not believe that making "gay coupling equal to heterosexual marriage" will shape a "more just and loving society," Andrew Lang, a "lay theologian," former journalist and current director of Internet Services for the UCC Office of Communication, disagrees. "The partner in a same-sex relationship is truly 'other'—not through the complementarity of a man and woman, of course, but in the mutuality of two persons who in freedom choose each other and delight in being chosen," he says. "God creates these relationships because, within the limits of our given sexuality, we are always called out of isolation into community. Always! Through these relationships we learn what it means to be truly human, to care for another as much as we care for ourselves, and to learn that a life enclosed on itself is death, but a life opened to other lives is God's gift and command to those who believe."

Andy invokes the Christian sense of responsible freedom as an argument in favor of the blessing of same-sex unions.[5] "Freedom, according to all Christian traditions, is not only freedom *from,* but also freedom *for,*" he continues. "It is in this [Christian] community, and nowhere else, that God meets me through Word and Sacrament, and where I learn the boundaries and, paradoxically, the unlimited possibilities of the freedom that is mine only as a gift, and never as self-determination. . . . We all sense that the scattered and broken pieces of our lives (and our relationships) belong together, but we simply don't know how to rebuild the structure we have demolished." And Christianity, Andy asserts, has a duty to provide structure to homosexual relationships—a similar kind of structure that Christianity provides in heterosexual marriages.

What does this duty mean for ministers? "The church's pastoral concern for these [gay and lesbian] couples necessarily requires the public, liturgical expression of the vows that bind them together," Andy continues. "Pastoral care without the public recognition of their vows would undermine the moral accountability of same-sex couples to each other and to the church. The congregation cannot legitimately expect conformity to ethical norms for same-sex partners if it is unwilling to witness the vows in which those partners commit themselves—in the presence of the community—to fidelity and mutual obedience. If a congregation permits pastoral care but denies the public rite of union, it is saying, in effect, 'We expect you to honor your covenant, but we don't want to hear about it outside the pastor's office.' 'Don't-ask-don't-tell' is a cruel way of life for same-sex couples, and if that constraint were imposed on heterosexual partners, I doubt that many marriages could survive. 'Private' promises of fidelity apart from the community are like New Year's resolutions—easy to break."

That the UCC is willing to consider issues involved in gay and lesbian partnerships is nowhere more apparent than the University Congregational United Church of Christ in Seattle, Washington, where Peter Ilgenfritz and David Shull, partners in a committed relationship, serve as pastors on the four-member clergy team. Whereas Peter is a "lifelong UCC member," David grew up in the Presbyterian Church. "Going to church every Sunday was always part of my life," Peter explains. "I felt that all people were welcomed into [the church I attended], whether they were doubters, seekers, or believers. That's what really kept me in that place. I felt welcomed and nurtured. Then, while attending Colgate University, I experienced a deep call to go into the ministry. I continued to grow in my faith throughout college. After graduating, I went directly to Yale Divinity School."

Unlike Peter, David never considered the professional ministry until after he graduated from college. In fact, he stopped attending church from the eighth grade until his junior year in college. "When I was nine years old, my family and I lived in India for a year," he explains. "I saw extreme poverty in that country, but listened to stories of the love and the justice of God every Sunday in church after coming back to the States. Skeptical of this 'loving God,' I refused to join the church. Why, I wondered openly in a confirmation class, would a loving God allow people to suffer? The answers to this question, I was told, were not ours to know. Realizing I didn't have a place to ask the kinds of questions I needed to ask, I stopped going to church."

During his junior year of college, David returned to church—the Metropolitan Memorial Methodist Church in Washington, D.C. There, he felt that the minister was talking directly to him. "This was a place where I was completely understood," he says. "That made me feel that a church could be a relevant place, after all."

After graduation, he worked in state government for a while and attended a large Presbyterian church in Columbus, Ohio. "I got involved in various things, like working with a middle school musical and attending a singles group," he says. "These people, coupled with my experiences living with two Roman Catholics, were the first people my age I encountered who lived their faith and weren't fundamentalists. I began to think I might be called to professional ministry. I entered Yale Divinity School. There, I met Peter in the fall of 1984. It was two thirds of the way through seminary that I discovered I was gay. This put me in a crisis for a number of reasons, not the least of which was that the Presbyterian Church would not ordain me if I were honest about my love for Peter. I went ahead with Presbyterian ordination and paid the price that comes when one's integrity is violated: I was sick most of the two years of my Presbyterian ministry in Pennsylvania."

After divinity school, David pastored in Pennsylvania, while Peter served a church in Ithaca, New York. "That was our coming-out time," Peter explains. "We came out to ourselves, to our families, and to our friends. Then, we lived in Chicago for five years. For a while, I directed a not-for-profit AIDS service organization, while David was a social worker. When we left our churches in New York and Pennsylvania, we lost our hope to return to the local church. In Chicago, David and I began talking about doing some ministry together. Finally, it became clear to both of us that we needed to get back into local church ministry. We wanted to do that together. Perhaps naively, and full of hopefulness, we felt a calling to apply, as a couple, to a church. We did just that—much against the advice of many friends and in spite of our feeling that this wasn't going to happen in our lifetimes."

In January 1993, David and Peter were chosen as pastoral candidates for a small church in Columbus, Ohio, but were ultimately voted down by the congregation—a decision that shattered them. "But we grew more determined," says Peter. "In the spring of 1993, I realized that although we wanted a church, perhaps our true calling was to knock on the door of the church and invite churches to face the issue of homosexuality and the gospel. We received over one hundred rejections by mid-1993. We were discouraged and decided, during a vacation that fall, to stop our search. When we returned home, we found three letters from search committees who wanted to learn more about us. One was from University Congregational United Church of Christ."

After the search committee listened to both men preach at a UCC church about ninety miles north of Seattle, David and Peter returned to Chicago, where they waited three weeks while two other candidates were reviewed. "The search committee told us to expect a call on Tuesday night," David recalls. "We stayed up and stayed up, and there was no call. Finally, we went to sleep, certain the search committee had offered the position to someone else and was waiting for a response before calling us."

The following morning, the phone rang. The committee chair told them the committee had not yet reached a decision. By evening, another call informed them they were the committee's first choice.

University's search process could easily serve as a model for other churches. "They could have written a book on how to do it well," David says. "They didn't get together to bring in a candidate who is gay, or a person of color, or a handicapped person. They came to the process seeking the best fit between church and pastor. The needs of the congregation and the unique gifts of the candidates needed to be a good match."

The search committee announced its recommendation of Peter and David a month before the couple would preach before the congregation, who would then vote. During that time, the search committee secured letters from university area churches, stating their willingness to continue ecumenical work with a church that had gay clergy. The search committee also sponsored question-and-answer sessions during which parishioners could share their reactions. Some expressed deep concern over calling a gay couple. "We flew in from Chicago five days before the vote," David continues. "One very helpful event that week was a question-and-answer period with two hundred people. This two-hour session allowed members to see us, not only as two gay men who are partnered, but also as human beings. That Sunday, we led the worship service. Over eight hundred people attended to worship in a sanctuary that seats six hundred people. It was just overwhelming.

"In our sermon, we named the elephant in the room," David continues. "We named the fears and concerns generated by the possibility of calling two gay pastors. We knew that people for whom this church was family probably feared the changes that might come about if we were called. Would this become a gay church? Would their friends leave? That was the first part of our sermon. Then, we lifted up the gospel's call to trust and to step into places of darkness and fear where we are called to walk with Christ. As Christians, we said, we are called to take risks."

After the sermon, the men waited at a parishioner's house while the congregation made its decision—a decision that took ninety minutes. During that time, a parishioner made a blanket statement condemning homosexuality. A seventy-one-year-old woman, respected and loved by the congregation, stood and announced: "Please watch what you're saying. You're talking about me, you know." From that moment on, the tone of the discussion shifted. Finally, 76 percent of the congregation approved calling Peter and David to serve as associate pastors. "We were stunned," recalls David. "Rev. [Gail] Crouch, another associate pastor at the church, gave us a big hug as we walked into the church. One concern was that some of the affluent, established people in the church would leave, causing significant financial problems for a large church. But in 1990, the congregation voted to be Open and Affirming. They were willing to put their money where their mouth was. Immediately after the vote, one family donated ten thousand dollars. They explained their reason: 'This is the kind of church we want to raise our kids in.' "

Out of twelve hundred parishioners, roughly sixteen people left. Some members expressed concern that University might become a "gay church." "At the time of our selection, there were only five openly gay or lesbian folks in the entire congregation," says David. "Now, perhaps 10 percent of our new members are gay and lesbian. Because Christianity has shown such hostility toward gays and lesbians, there is not a slew of them wanting to return."

A tremendous amount of publicity resulted from their invitation. "We appeared on the front page of the *Seattle Times,* and there was a story in *USA Today,*" Peter says. "What was interesting is that while we experienced no controversy in our church, the media seemed intent on creating some. The press kept going to the pastor of a large fundamentalist church in town. Of course, his reaction to our selection was not positive. In my view, the press used him to create drama."

In the beginning, Peter and David encountered some difficulty in working so closely together. "For the first couple of years, I found myself feeling competitive," David explains. "For example, I wondered why some parishioners preferred to confide in Peter rather than in me. So there was some clear tension we had to deal with."

"We rapidly established some very clear boundaries," adds Peter. "We don't talk about church when we're at home together. At church, we're part of a larger staff. We have two clergy colleagues; we work in different areas."

Don MacKenzie, head of staff, encouraged an evolution of ministry that is egalitarian, not hierarchical. "For the past two years, the four of us have established a team ministry," Peters says. "Each of the clergy shares equally in leadership. Each preaches 25 percent of the time. We know what we do well; we use our talents and strengths to the benefit of the church."

Prior to their relocation from Chicago, David and Peter had considered the prospect of adoption. "We built a lot of excitement around that possibility," David says. "But now, we've realized that isn't something we can do. Our work here is very demanding. We don't have enough time for a child right now. So we are grateful to have so many children at church in our lives.

We keep learning better ways to make room to be ourselves, and we have room to grow. If we had ended up in a small church—the two of us sharing the responsibilities of one minister without clergy colleagues—that would have been a disaster."

In the beginning, Peter says, he felt as though he could never fit the pieces of his life together. "My deep sense of ministry has always been the focus of my life," he says. "But once we accepted the call to University, my love of God, my love of Dave, and my deep sense of ministry have all come together. I feel richly blessed."

Among mainline Christian denominations, UCC unquestionably remains the most inclusive, tenaciously following, as its faith statements allege, the precept that finding characteristics that unite human beings is infinitely more Christ-like than focusing on issues that separate and alienate.

There is, however, another denomination where ministers of all Christian traditions can find a home—and gay and lesbian Christians can find their spiritual needs addressed without dissension and debate. It is a denomination whose invitation to gays and lesbians is unconditional.

What the Heart Says

In 1968, nine months before the Stonewall Rebellion in Greenwich Village that marked the beginning of the modern gay and lesbian civil rights movement, Troy Perry founded the Universal Fellowship of Metropolitan Community Churches (UFMCC) to answer the need among gays and lesbians for positive, affirming houses of worship. Over the past thirty years, UFMCC has grown to more than fifty-two thousand members; in fact, it is the largest gay and lesbian organization in the United States. Its statement of faith does not deviate from the traditional belief in a triune God or in the human capacity for salvation through a belief in Jesus Christ. The most significant difference between a UFMCC church and any other Protestant church is that UFMCC's congregations are largely gay and lesbian.

Perry began his ministry in the Pentecostal tradition. (Because that influence is often apparent in the style of UFMCC services, many gay and lesbian Christians are uncomfortable there.) On several occasions, he has been a guest of the White House. In 1998, the UFMCC received a one-hundred-thousand dollar grant from the Ford Foundation designated to establish support programs for at-risk gay and lesbian youth.

The UFMCC continues to grow by leaps and bounds.

Though Perry has earned the respect of many people, from parishioners to presidents, his ministry began modestly with service to congregations in Georgia, Florida, Alabama, and Illinois affiliated with the Tennessee-based Church of God. All the while, questions about his sexual orientation perplexed him. Finally, he confessed the alarming suspicion to a church mentor. "All you need is a good woman," the mentor advised.

Perry married the man's daughter.

Then, at the age of twenty-three, while serving as pastor of the Church of God of Prophecy in Santa Ana, California, he told a superior that he was gay. In short order, the denomination excommunicated him. His wife bailed out of their marriage, taking their two sons, ages three and one, with her.

Perry succumbed to a life of promiscuity. "I was a homosexual; I was gonna die and go to hell," he says. "So I figured I might as well bust hell wide open."[6]

After a suicide attempt precipitated by the unexpected end of a relationship, a short stint in the army, and a few years working as a salesman, Perry returned to church.

Well, not just any church. At the coaxing of his mother and a neighborhood psychic, he decided to start his own religious movement. Only twelve people attended his first service. However, news of this gay-friendly church quickly spread through magazine, newspaper, and television coverage.

Despite the overwhelming success of the church he founded—in 1997, the UFMCC paid almost four million dollars for a West Hollywood complex slated to serve as the denomination's worldwide headquarters—one component of his life still causes him pain. He hasn't spoken to his ex-wife in thirty-five years. "It's one of those things," he says. "I just have to leave it alone. My ex-wife and oldest son have made it clear they do not want me to contact them. It still bothers me, but I have to respect their wishes."

However, in 1984, James Michael Perry, his youngest son, contacted him, then asked his father to officiate at his wedding. "My perception of my father growing up, from what my mother had told me, was that he was an evil man, that homosexuality was the devil's work," James said. "Now that I know him, I'm proud of what he's done. I don't understand homosexuals, but I don't think gay jokes are funny anymore. I'm different now, thanks to my father."

Many gay and lesbian ministers feel overwhelming gratitude to Perry. Because of the UFMCC, they can choose between a traditional denomination, which probably means witnessing from the closet or from a political battleground, or the UFMCC, where their major role will be to lead congregations on their spiritual journeys.

Jim Richards was originally ordained in the Presbyterian Church in 1961. "I came to this denomination (UFMCC) as pastor in October 1992," Jim, whose church is located in Knoxville, Tennessee, explains. "When I was credentialed in 1995 for ordination in the UFMCC, I chose to have my Presbyterian ordination acknowledged rather than being re-ordained. I want the Presbyterians to know that their ordination continues in my ministry to gays and lesbians."

In a way, Jim's life in the closet forced him to leave the Presbyterian Church (U.S.A.). "I was arrested while I was a Presbyterian minister," he confesses. "That created an opportunity for newspapers to publicly out me. I chose to join the UFMCC church that I had been attending, surreptitiously, for five years, in Topeka. Joining another church was required in order to begin the process of transferring my credentials from PC(USA). As a matter of policy, the PC(USA) erased my name from the roll because I had joined another denomination. No action was ever taken against me related to the arrest or the circumstantial evidence that I was gay. My ordination could not be removed without a trial. Removing my name from the rolls made any further action impossible."

On October 19, 1994, Jim was arrested in an adult theater for touching a fully-clothed, undercover detective on the leg. "I was charged with simple battery," he says. "The fact that it happened in an adult theater hit the newspapers. At that point, the Presbyterians chose to remove me from the church that I was serving. I was not free to participate in ministerial tasks until the investigation was completed. But by joining a church of another denomination, I had 'renounced the jurisdiction' of the Presbyterian Church."

In large part, Jim's arrest in the adult theater was the consequence of a "deeply mystical experience" he had as a young adolescent, when denial of his homosexuality began. He internalized the predominant social message that homosexuality was evil. "I was confronted by Jesus Christ when I was only twelve," he explains. "I believed I had been called to the ministry. Sure that God would not call a homosexual, I believed, therefore, that I must not be gay. I began sublimating anything having to do with homosexuality. I practiced very hard the business of acting masculine. In all honesty, I went through my college and seminary education, and close to twenty-five years of ministry, believing I was straight."

In fact, Jim and his wife, Ann, spent thirty-one years together and had three children. "She herself is an ordained Presbyterian minister," he continues. "During the years she was raising our children, she stayed home and cared for them. I have a vested pension in the church. Upon my death or retirement, her pension will not support her. That's why there will be no divorce unless she seeks it, so that she will have retirement income. Ann, who lives in Portland, Oregon, and I have an amiable relationship. We spend time together. As a couple, we also spend time with our children. In fact, Ann has been very badly treated because of her continued friendship with me. But she has always stood by me and, in fact, identifies, in her preaching, issues of the gay and lesbian community as something the church should address. She speaks publicly in support of the ordination of gays and lesbians." (In January 1999, Ann and Jim finally got a divorce when the Presbyterian Pension Plan agreed to abide by a divorce decree that stipulated transferring pension credits from Jim's plan to Ann's, sufficient to make the two retirement programs equal.)

Now in his early sixties, Jim self-identified as gay when he was in his mid-forties. "Before I came out to myself, I was an activist in civil rights issues in the 1960s and opposed the Vietnam conflict," he says. Then, because of his experience as an advisor to the Kansas City Council regarding the city's rapid race to franchise a less-than-scrupulous cable television company, the UCC asked him to assume responsibilities as Deputy Director of Communication. "That occurred in the 1970s. I agreed, as long as I wasn't expected to switch denominations. During my tenure, we accomplished landmark work, including new rules for fairness to women and Blacks in broadcasting. The UCC Office of Communication's action against a television station in Jackson, Mississippi, for 'failure to broadcast in the public interest,' relative to racial language on the air and programming practices, resulted in the station owners' loss of their broadcast license."

However, reaching an acceptable comfort level with his homosexuality required much more effort than tackling social and political issues. "As I said, I had decided that God wouldn't call a homosexual to ministry," he explains. "I was sure being a homosexual was not good. I am a liberal person. I had always been one who would say that 'some of my best friends are gay,' and that was quite literally true. I was never threatened by homosexuality in general—just my own."

In his early relationship with Ann, Jim lived quite easily in his role as a heterosexual man. "Ann had grown up in a home where sex was dirty," he explains. "She was the perfect person for me to get close to. She was a great date who didn't expect—or want—sex from me. I didn't have any trouble being goody-goody-two-shoes, which is why, I thought, I didn't want sex with her. That was in our college years at a little Presbyterian college in Emporia, Kansas. Upon graduation, she went to a California seminary, and I to one in Chicago. I wasn't interested in marriage then, and now I know why."

Ann and Jim crossed paths again when she came to visit her parents in Kansas City. "I was serving a summer internship in a Kansas City church," Jim explains. "We got together several times, and at the end of the period, I proposed to her. A minister needs to be married, right? We were enormously compatible in every way. We still had never had sex."

During the intervening years, Ann had married a seminary classmate. That marriage was annulled within a month or two. Evidently, he, too, was gay, and unable to consummate the marriage. "With great disappointment, she reacted to my self-discovery. She and I both got into therapy. She began to deal with the implications of being married, yet again, to a gay man. She has always enjoyed the company of gay men, I know that. But I don't know how well she has dealt with what this means. [Our relationship] worked so beautifully in college. We loved to dance with each other. In fact, we still do."

While attending seminary, Jim "flunked the Rorschach Test. Jokingly, I always put it that way. They made me take it again. I sensed that homosexuality was what it was all about. I saw too many penises and not enough vaginas. During the re-test, I was very careful to see more vaginas."

Some gay and lesbian mainline ministers perceive the UFMCC to be segregationist and fear that it communicates to both parishioners and clergy that gays and lesbians have gifts that are valuable only to one another. "I think that perspective is not fair," Jim says. "In fact, here in Knoxville, a number of my members go to both places—the Baptist church, for example, in the morning; then at night, they come to MCC. These are folks who would not be welcome in their home church if the congregation there knew they are gay. But they come to our services in the evening so they can express their faith and make that expression of faith with their partners. Occasionally, I pick up from the gay community that UFMCC has a reputation as a cruise place. That always comes from people who have never worshiped with us, who are surprised that we don't have sex on the altar. I'm very comfortable with my Presbyterian background; it is not compromised here. No denominational tradition is. Rather than saying UFMCC is segregationist, I would say that it is inclusive in ways other churches are not. We give Methodists, for example, the freedom to worship the same God and Jesus Christ while being open about their sexuality, which is what the straight folks are doing every Sunday morning."

In addition to the freedom to worship in a faith community that affirms their identity in wholeness, gays and lesbians should have the right to marry. "I'm very positive about marriage," Jim says. One objection many heterosexuals have to same-sex marriage derives from their perception of gays and lesbians as promiscuous and incapable of establishing long-term commitments. "Of course, I think monogamy is very important, and something that all Christians ought to strive for," Jim says. "Straights have even asked: 'What do you say to gays about all their promiscuity?' And I say to them: 'What do you say about yours? I wish I could introduce you to the couples in my congregation who have been together thirty-five years, twenty-eight years, twenty-five years, twenty-two. . . .' So many long-term relationships! Is there promiscuity in the gay community? You bet. Is there promiscuity in the Presbyterian Church down the street? You bet. Is that good? No! But it is not different."

Like other ministers, Jim experiences an occasional sense of alienation, even in the inclusive UFMCC church. "I have to combat that," he admits. "The gay community is damned angry about the way the church has treated them. No other group, I think, is as angry as the gay community toward the injustices often perpetrated in the name of Christianity. One joyful experience that I have fairly regularly is watching people discover that UFMCC offers the same gospel as the church down the street. But we are willing to say, '*You, too,* are accepted and loved.'"

The tide of ex-gay ministry ads, both in newspapers and on television, is a "tragedy and a travesty." "I have no doubt they have paved the way for innumerable suicides," Jim says. "We have a so-called transformative ministry in Knoxville that operates out of Christ Chapel. But when I served in the Presbyterian Church in Topeka, Kansas, members of the Menninger family—the founders of the famed psychiatric clinic—and members of the Menninger staff were also members of my congregation. So was the head of the sex-therapy department. When I was doing some public speaking on the subject of homosexuality, I asked him for a quotable quote."

"It's biological. It's genetic. It's inherited," the therapist responded, identifying the "causes of homosexuality."

"I asked him if he had ever dealt with someone who was acting out a homosexual lifestyle but was not gay," Jim continues. "Only once, he said, aside from prisoners in jail. This man was terribly handicapped and deformed. He was involved in a homosexual 'lifestyle' because that's all he had available to him. So, based on the views of this scientist and my own self-knowledge, I don't have any respect at all for the ex-gay movement. I think it is quite possible to change one's behavior, but it is not possible to change one's orientation. And when a person thinks he or she has been 'cured' and continues to be attracted to same-gender persons, guilt feelings can build to suicidal levels. Some people live, as I did until my midforties, a straight lifestyle, but I wasn't straight then, and I'm not straight now. And I would say that here in the hills of East Tennessee, lots of young people are pretending to be straight because they think their lives would be threatened any other way."

Soon after Jim moved to Knoxville, a young man stopped by his office. "I have to find a place to live and a job," he said. "I'm gay, and my mother carries a .357-magnum in her purse. She told me she will blow the brains out of any faggot. My grandmother has discovered that I'm gay and threatens to tell Mom herself unless I do by the end of the month."

Later, however, the young man discovered his mother already knew of his sexual orientation. "She was trying to scare it out of him," Jim says, "hoping that, through fear, he would 'go straight.'"

In the 1950s, while Jim attended seminary, circumstances, although not as threatening as the young parishioner perceived his situation to be, were very repressive. "One student on campus—I had no question he was gay—just disappeared one night," Jim says. "The next morning, he was nowhere to be found. Later, I discovered what happened. The Dean of Students had found out my friend was gay and told him he wasn't qualified to become a Presbyterian minister." Quietly, and under the cloak of darkness, the young man had moved out.

Originally from New Orleans, Leslie Addison, a UFMCC minister in Oakland, California, says that the Metropolitan Community Church provides wonderful support in the coming-out process, particularly in small towns. "Our church is clearly identified as a friendly space," she explains. "Let me give a very sad example. Recently, a friend of mine died from AIDS. His family were members of the Reformed Church in Iowa. Two different memorial services were held for him. The minister at the Reformed Church did not say anything about AIDS. There, his parents couldn't have admitted their son was gay or even that he had AIDS. Their grief had to be experienced in a repressive faith community, one that was in denial. On the other hand, his friends and partner had to experience their loss and say their good-byes in the UFMCC. It's shameful that one's lover and one's parents can't even grieve in the same place."

That many churches equate homosexuality to sin—like theft, greed, covetousness, or gluttony—really goads Leslie. "Once, at a church supply store in Baton Rouge, I stood at a clothing rack, where I found a belt as long as I am tall," she says. "I asked the salesperson if she had ever sold a belt that large. She told me that most people who buy belts that huge are fundamentalist preachers. I wondered, if I attended any of the churches where these guys preached, whether I would hear as many sermons about gluttony as I have already heard from their pulpits about homosexuality. The answer is no, of course not. I will believe that those ministers who say homosexuality is a sin really believe what they are saying when they treat all other sins as they treat homosexuality. What's so basic to me, and yet seems so complicated for them to grasp, is that being a lesbian isn't about who I have sex with, but who I love. Love is one of the central messages of Jesus. His ministry is about the vastness and the fullness of that love. It's sad when my brothers and sisters are no longer welcomed in their communities of faith because their church doctrine is not big enough for them."

Neither are some traditions "big enough" for gay and lesbian ministers to continue in service to their congregations. "When gay and lesbian ministers are removed from the service of their churches, they are removed very, very quickly," Leslie explains. "Part of the reason for such quick expulsion is that church leaders have to get them out of the pulpit as quickly as possible. Otherwise, the congregation might see God working in and through that gay or lesbian pastor." Leslie sighs. "There are times when I just don't understand heterosexuals."

In the perception of Thomas Bohache, a UFMCC minister in Delaware, few significant differences exist between homosexuals and heterosexuals. In high school, however, Tom was a stranger to that realization. "I felt a calling to ministry in the Roman Catholic priesthood while I was growing up," he explains. "I wanted to do God's work. At some point in parochial school, I was struck by the disturbing notion that God did not love me. That was what I believed at the time. That belief was the result of priests and nuns indicating that 'some things'—like homosexuality—weren't to be talked about. As a result, I left the Catholic Church when I was nineteen. It broke my heart because I wanted so much to be a priest. But priesthood was not an option for me. I didn't go anywhere near a church for five or six years. If God wanted no part of me, then I wanted no part of God."

After finishing a bachelor's degree at UCLA, Tom visited a local Metropolitan Community Church. "I was suspicious of it," he admits. "I wondered why all these queers were playing church."

Then, in 1985, a young man Tom was dating died from AIDS complications. "His death turned my life around," he says. "Basically, here's what happened. I went to his bedside. He knew I had grown up in a religious household and that currently I was attending UFMCC. His mother's priest had been there earlier and had told him he was going to hell and that AIDS had been God's punishment for his sins. So he asked me to pray for him." Tom pauses. It is difficult for him to continue. "I told him he—he could pray, too. He didn't need *me* to pray for him. But he was convinced that God wouldn't listen to his prayers. The next time I visited, he had pneumocystis pneumonia [lung infection sometimes occurring in immunosuppressed people]. Weakly, he squeezed my hand."

"I did it," he said, smiling.

"Did what?" Tom asked.

"I prayed."

It was the last time Tom saw him alive.

"After his death, I became even more involved in the UFMCC. Rather than turning away from God, I turned toward my faith. If I could help just one more person who had that feeling of helplessness—of hopelessness—then that accomplishment would be wonderful," Tom says.

Tom rejects a narrow view of human sexuality—that its sole divine purpose is procreation. "Sexuality is the expression of love," he says. "In Genesis, when God creates a human being, God creates humanity in God's own image. Clearly, the union of the first humans was about companionship—not about procreation." Then, when Adam and Eve were disobedient to God's Word, they became alienated from their sexuality. "That alienation causes people to feel shameful," Tom explains. "Adam and Eve felt our bodies should be covered up. I believe that salvation, which is the undoing of sin, is a way to synthesize the sexual and spiritual. If we see our spiritual home being shattered by the first sin, then we accept God through our salvation. That's God's way of bringing our sexuality back into wholeness. That's why I get really irritated when religious people talk about 'practicing' homosexuals being worse than 'nonpracticing' ones. That kind of rhetoric encourages us to keep our lives in a state of further disintegration."

In fact, to curb spiritual disintegration, gay men and lesbians must strive to trust themselves, their feelings, and their values. They must trust their conviction that their love enjoys God's approval, too. "Gays and lesbians must learn to trust their experience of the divine," he says. "We must realize that our experience is just as valid as anyone else's. Basically, it all comes down to an issue of worthiness. It's important to realize that sexuality is a gift; gays and lesbians are created to be exactly who we are."

But of most importance, Tom says, the UFMCC answers the question of whether God really loves gay and lesbian Christians. "To find that answer—to be sure of it—takes a lot of work," he says. "One incident can send us reeling back. I'm a perfect example of that. When my boyfriend was dying, I was very new to UFMCC. But I remember calling my pastor and asking her if Tony had died because I had stopped coming to church."

Many experiences can send Christians "reeling back" into shadows of doubt and disillusion. Reconciliation has the capacity to guide Christians toward a greater purpose. Patricia Voelker, UFMCC pastor in Columbia, South Carolina, and the first openly lesbian Christian chaplain at the University of South Carolina, left the Methodist Church because her new pastor was a racist. "That was only one of his disruptive, damaging characteristics," she says. "I left organized religion for ten years—one of the best gifts I ever gave myself!"

Patricia's first experience in the UFMCC was not positive. "My first visit to St. Joan of Arc MCC (now MCC-Charleston) introduced me to a layman who would later become a dear friend," she explains. "It also introduced me to a less-than-familiar form of communion. The male pastor and his assistant invited the congregation to come forward. They did so, individually or as couples. He extended his arms and placed his hands on their backs as they knelt. To my uninitiated eyes, the gesture was a reminder of Dracula receiving his next victim. The pastor whispered in the congregants' ears, then kissed them on the mouth! I was raised in a church where communion plates were passed down the pews, and I wanted nothing to do with this too-intimate process. Later, UFMCC's open communion—without the intimate kiss—became the most wonderful part of worship for me. Still that memory stays with me, and, as celebrant now, I intentionally use language that describes our manner of communion, complete with personal prayer at the altar. I also offer the congregant the option of receiving communion another way if personal prayer is invasive. As a survivor of sexual abuse, I emphasize the need to be careful in how we touch one another, even in this holy moment of oneness."

Before acknowledging a call to ministry, Patricia taught public school for seventeen years. Finally, she could no longer ignore God's voice. She left her classroom behind, only to become a student once again. "I took some correspondence courses and attended classes in other districts to meet requirements in Bible, sexuality, UFMCC polity, and so forth," she says of the ordination process. "I left Charleston at the end of 1990 for the 'student clergy' part of preparation for ministry. This internship involved serving two years with a supervising pastor at a church in Denton, Texas. I completed all the course work and three two-week sessions of 'Orientation to Pastoring' during those two years."

Since 1994, Patricia has become the Columbia area's "lesbian du jour." "One of the most exciting invitations came early in 1998, when the youth minister of a nearby United Methodist church invited us [various gay and lesbian Christians, both parishioners and church leaders] to speak to the youth group about being gay and Christian," she explains. "There were fifteen youth, three parents, the youth minister, the associate pastor, and another volunteer present. There were seventeen of us. The youth said all the things we might have said, but it was so much more effective coming from them. They asked their own leadership why the Methodists say, 'all persons have sacred worth,' then reject gays. One young man said to the associate pastor, 'In other words, we will ordain liars, but not homosexuals.'"

Like many middle-aged gay and lesbian people, Patricia faced a long process of coming to grips with her orientation. Despite today's many challenges and controversies, society was even tougher on gays and lesbians when she was growing up. "I wasn't aware of being a lesbian when I was married and didn't know it until I was thirty-nine," she says. (Patricia and her ex-husband were married for two years. Though she hasn't seen her ex-husband since they divorced in 1963, she enjoys a "wonderful" relationship with her daughter.) "When I grew up in the 1950s, there were limited role models. I wasn't allowed into a group of women I now believe to have been lesbians. That made it a lot harder for me to know [about myself]. Today, there are so many varied images of gays and lesbians. No one has to fit a stereotype. With my internal rearview mirror, I see I have always been a lesbian. I don't consider myself to have been closeted, however, so much as unaware of the possibility of being anything except heterosexual. Today, people find that hard to believe. If they'd grown up in the 1950s, they might understand more easily."

In 1979, Patricia began a friendship with a woman that culminated in a mutual acknowledgment of their love. "She was terrified to call it what it was, and we danced around the reality," Patricia says. "That is a closet. I was lucky that God opened the closet door for me. The feelings I had for her were clearly more than friendship. Then, in one moment, clarity struck. And it struck me spiritually, with a sense of total access to God. There was this moment in time—I know it was only a moment—but it had the sense of being timeless. Intellectually, I knew that if I had asked anything of the universe, the answer would have been given to me. I was that intimate with the All. For me, it was as if God rejoiced, 'Finally, she's going to be who she's supposed to be.' We, All and I, were in celebration. The One and I, the cosmos and I."

Patricia believes that the UFMCC delivers a theological message that is difficult for mainline traditions to grasp. "The very fact that we say everyone is created in God's image, and God didn't create junk—that separates us right there," she asserts. "We don't build a hierarchy of sinners. That's what you hear in the other churches. We believe that you can truly be in a spiritual relationship with God and be who you are sexually. That is different. We have figured out that God really *does* love everyone and that liberation theology frees heterosexuals, too. Not all of our members are homosexual, but most are. Some bring family members who are heterosexual. The freedom to be should be a gift to everybody."

Recently, Patricia met Marcus Borg, author of *Meeting Jesus Again, for the First Time*. When Patricia identified herself as a UFMCC pastor, Borg alluded to his appearances at several UFMCC churches on the west coast.

"I know it's not UFMCC's mission, but if those who think gays and lesbians can't be Christian would just attend a worship service, they'd feel God's presence," he said.

"I love it when others affirm what I've found in our worship services," Patricia says. "It's that joy of being as God intended us to be that is liberating, not only to us, but to everyone."

In 1996, Patricia addressed a South Carolina legislative committee regarding a bill—which passed into law—forbidding recognition of same-sex marriages, even if other states legalized them. "My testimony told the stories of two couples," she explains. "When one partner in the first couple died, the surviving member automatically began receiving social security, insurance benefits, respect as the bereaved, full and unobstructed access to belongings and funeral arrangements. With the second couple, the surviving member immediately lost income, access to that person's belongings, the ability to even plan funeral arrangements. The first were my mother and father. The second were two men I know. These gay men had done all the things that a heterosexual couple had done as a family unit; yet without legal rights, the surviving gay partner was put at financial risk."

It is precisely this political component of her ministry that places Patricia as the occasional subject of letters to the editor of the local newspaper. "Some letters have said I'm leading my congregation to hell," she says. "But my home phone number is listed in the directory. I've received only one negative call. My approach toward those people who have fundamentalist attitudes is quite simple, and I suggest others use the same approach. Ask yourself: Is this fundamentalist a person I want to have a relationship with? If it is, then you interact with that individual. You either agree not to talk about the issues of homosexuality—except within some safe guidelines—or you try to get into a nonthreatening dialog toward the goal of finding where his or her fear is. If the person is standing on a street corner during a Pride Parade and you won't see him or her again, you may react differently. But the minute you start a debate on scripture with someone whose mind is closed, you have lost. It's fine to argue, if all you want to do is expend some energy. But what's even better is reading and exploring the Bible—not for verbal jousting with somebody, but to have some degree of comfort when you are challenged."

Visionary faith communities acknowledge scripture as morally and spiritually grounded—a compass from God, yet not a map to heaven. However, as with any compass, the wholeness of meaning is not implicit in the readings. To understand the implications fully, people of faith use God's gifts of mind and compassion, of conscience and justice, to make decisions resonating with the soundness of reason, forgiveness, mercy, and grace.

Yet movement toward full affirmation of gay and lesbian Christians, whether laity or leadership, paves the way not only for "verbal jousting" but also for divisions in faith communities that could hardly have been predicted until several years ago. If fault lines, created by rumblings over gay and lesbian issues, continue to expand, what will the future hold for Christianity in America?

5

REFORMATION 2000

Freedom Struggle

Now, I find myself looking back, once again, to the beginning—the beginning of awareness of my homosexual orientation, the beginning of my meager witness to the "Everlasting Yes" of a Christianity that could embrace me. I recall, once again, the churches I have attended where I felt affirmed. Yet all along, I knew, as strongly as I ever experienced faith in Christ, that the love of many of my fellow Christians was conditional. Once, I was a closeted teacher. I *would* have been a closeted minister, had I married Claire and performed all the roles the ELCA would have expected of me. For years, I have been a closeted Christian. But now, after all that I have filtered into these pages, I am still perplexed that my orientation—an orientation that has defined and established the depth of my love—could cause controversy for Christianity. Like most gay men and lesbians, I am a person with morals. I am a person with a capacity to love—a capacity that *must* have limits; but, in all honesty, I have not found them yet. I am a person with talents, abilities, and insights that are no better—but certainly no worse—than those of my heterosexual brothers and sisters. I am a person whose love for Josh, my partner, deserves the acknowledgment, blessing, and recognition that heterosexual relationships deserve. I am a person who fought hard to feel deserving of God's love and acceptance—*just as I am.*

On Palm Sunday weekend, Josh and I visited my parents, who were entertaining two of my aunts—one of whom was Aunt Sadie, my arsenal of jokes that kept me popular before my "conversion experience." For a brief fifteen minutes, we chatted about the "gay issue" in Christianity. Although my parents and my aunts try very hard—and with much success, I'm proud to say—to understand the issues, Aunt Nell, who attends an Episcopal church, related an encounter that I found compelling and disturbing. Several weeks earlier, she had phoned her brother, my uncle, who had recently read a novel I wrote about an adolescent coming to terms with his homosexuality. My uncle, a Southern Baptist, wanted to know what Aunt Nell thought of the book.

"Well, I enjoyed it," she told him, then quickly changed the subject.

Why? I wanted to know. Even the thought of discussing homosexuality with him made her uncomfortable. What made her even more uncomfortable was the possibility that he might condemn me.

On the drive back to Charleston, it dawned on me that one reason—perhaps the primary reason—faith traditions are presently experiencing a difficult time with "this issue" is that no one wants to talk about it—about us. No one wants to talk about us because no one really knows *how*. That silence is perhaps the most injurious component of the controversy. Churches are reluctant to talk *with* us because it is easier to frame the issues without consideration of what we, as gay men and lesbians, know about ourselves. When we are silenced, the lies are easier to believe. Once lies are translated into beliefs, then church hierarchies impose silence.

Because of frequent institutional reluctance to encourage dialog before taking a stand, alienation undermines the sense of unity essential for faith communities to flourish. Precisely because we want to experience Christian unity, a growing number of us come out in acknowledgment of our faith and of our sexual orientation. However, a denomination's insistence that we keep our identities concealed—or keep our loving partnerships secret, locked away in shame and shadows—prolongs an inevitable confrontation. Anything other than worship in full acclamation of our identity is hypocrisy. We *feel* that conviction—our truth—as strongly as fundamentalists demonize us. However, church leaders all too often compromise their honest positions to maintain a temporary equilibrium. They fear that affirming us might encourage a great exodus from the pews. As a result, questions about church survival bedevil almost every mainline denomination.

Do congregations welcome, openly and unconditionally, gay and lesbian Christians into their churches? Can self-confident and "unrepentant" homosexuals even *be* Christian?

How do Christians interpret, in faith, love, and integrity, the biblical passages used most frequently to condemn homosexuality?

What is the wholly Christian stance concerning the alleged potential of gays and lesbians to be transformed into heterosexuality? Is such a transformation something people of faith should even desire, particularly if it means unhappiness or hypocrisy among fellow Christians?

What does it mean, this idea of hating the sin while loving the sinner? Are gays and lesbians truthful when they say their spirituality cannot be severed from their sexuality? If such extrication is not possible, might Christians need to revisit the idea—an idea with tremendous capacity for polarization within congregations—that homosexuality is a sin? If sin separates human beings from God, what is to be made of those gay and lesbian Christians who lead good and godly lives?

Can straight men and women trust the conviction, strong among gays and lesbians, that homosexuals are no different from heterosexuals, except in the way they physically express love to their partners?

What of marriage? Is it a sacrament that must, at all costs, be reserved for a man and a woman in love, or is that restriction merely camouflage for continued heterocentrism? Is the love between same sex partners equal to the love between opposite sex partners?

Are congregations willing to offer their pulpits to gay and lesbian clergy? If so, should parishioners demand celibacy of them? Or should congregations acknowledge and celebrate loving, long-term commitments between pastors and their same-sex spouses?

As a result of difficult questioning—questioning with no clear-cut resolution—most denominations have crash-landed in the middle of a controversy they feel has been forced upon them by the kind of cultural changes against which they are often insulated. And lest churches find themselves combating an expanding rift that resists all efforts to reverse it, they must handle the perplexing controversy with caution—a controversy, says journalist Bob Reeves ("Lifelong Commitments," *Lincoln Journal-Star,* February 7, 1998), that is more divisive than any other issue facing Christianity.

"Most churches say they welcome all people, regardless of sexual orientation," he writes. "But when a gay or lesbian couple wants to make a lifelong commitment in the presence of God, they find few priests or ministers willing to perform such a ceremony."

Indeed, because of the United Church of Christ's "prohomosexual" position, which grants pastoral autonomy to make a decision to perform same-sex holy union ceremonies, several congregations have seceded from the denomination (*Lincoln Journal-Star,* February 7, 1998). The possibility of still more secessions continues to increase, since Paul H. Sherry, President of the UCC, issued his "Now, No Condemnation" pastoral letter to all UCC congregations. "In my role as pastor to the UCC, and in this season of theological reflection on 'The Inclusive Church,' I offer this pastoral letter to remind all of us that the church is to be a place where all are welcomed, where the gifts of all are recognized and received, and where the rights of all are defended and promoted," he wrote in November 1998. "When so many in our society would reject and exclude, it is critical that we of the United Church of Christ bear witness to the conviction that it is possible to be deeply faithful to the Bible, profoundly respectful of the historic faith of the church and of its sacraments, and at the same time support the full inclusion and participation of all God's children in the membership and ministry of the church." In many ways, Sherry asserted, the UCC has been simultaneously "confronted and gifted." "We have been confronted and gifted by the presence in our church of gay, lesbian, and bisexual Christians who have been baptized in our sanctuaries, confirmed before our altars, and ordained by our associations," his letter continued. "We have been confronted and gifted by parents and grandparents, sisters and brothers, daughters and sons, faithful members of our church, whose embrace by a loving God has enabled them to accept a gay, lesbian, or bisexual family member, and who yearn for that same loving embrace to be extended by the church to their child, their grandchild, their brother or sister, their parent. We have been confronted and gifted by ordained men and women who have served faithfully and well for many years and who now wish to minister among us with renewed vitality, openly affirming their same-gender orientation. We have been confronted and gifted by gay, lesbian, and bisexual persons who have found love in the physical, emotional, and spiritual embrace of another, and are living in committed covenantal relationships of fidelity and trust which they yearn for the church to bless and the society to respect and protect."

As some faith communities struggled to determine whether they could accept gay and lesbian parishioners and pastors into Christian celebration—and if so, under what conditions—others challenged sensibilities through their encouragement of long-term, loving romantic commitments via same-sex holy unions or commitment ceremonies. Faith communities restricting opportunities for the blessing of same-sex partnerships often expressed outrage and indignation at what they perceived to be blatant defiance of centuries of tradition. "Unheard of twenty years ago," writes Kay Harvey (*St. Paul Pioneer Press,* February 15, 1998), "commitment ceremonies between gay and lesbian couples have become increasingly common."

Gary Kowalski, a Unitarian Universalist minister, blesses about three same-sex unions a year (*New York Times,* April 17, 1998). "The reason I perform same-sex ceremonies," he said, "is I think churches and other social institutions should be in the business of encouraging long-term relationships." Other ministers who performed these ceremonies cited more personal reasons. Rosie Olmstead performs as many as three unions a month within the More Light network in the PC(USA) and in the Open and Affirming network within the UCC. Gay couples who ask her to bless their unions "are seeking a public place in the community, a community larger than their closest friends, to say we expect this relationship to last," she says.

Pressures on churches to acknowledge gay and lesbian relationships have intensified. "Gays and lesbians fighting for greater legal acceptance in American society are finding allies and a warm welcome in an increasing number of religious communities," writes Diego Ribadeneira in the *Boston Globe* ("The Spiritual Life: Gay Marriages Gaining Allies in Many Religious Communities," February 14, 1998). "Many religious activists have embraced the cause of gay rights, including the right to marry, as a way of acting on their biblically-based belief in social justice and human dignity."

Ken Kirkey, co-chairman of the Boston chapter of "Freedom to Marry," told Ribadeneira that the issue of gay and lesbian marriage resonates with many religious leaders. "Why? Because it supports love. It supports family," he explains. "One minister said to me that we live in an era when the best psychological, sociological, and anthropological evidence shows that sexual orientation is morally neutral, so how can we say to a whole class of people that we're going to leave them on the outside?"

One answer to Kirkey's question is not hard to find in a culture where hate crimes against gays and lesbians are increasing in frequency and severity. Religious fundamentalism is morphing into religious vigilantism "before our very eyes." According to the National Gay and Lesbian Task Force, fourteen cities reported almost twenty-five hundred episodes of antigay harassment and violence in 1997, and a "sixty-seven percent increase in bomb threats and bombings to the gay, lesbian, bisexual, and transgendered community. This is terrorism. It is akin to the lynchings and cross-burnings during and after Reconstruction."[1]

In response to antigay tactics that depend on violence or lies and half-truths, gays, lesbians, and their heterosexual allies have positioned themselves on the front lines of a freedom struggle. "But for this freedom struggle to triumph, all of us must organize peacefully against the forces on the right who want to turn this democracy of ours into a theocracy of theirs," asserts *The Progressive.*

Yet, as schism's shadow looms ominously on the horizon, Christians with a desire to keep their denominations intact might exercise restraint in their response to the "other side." Is it fair, or even accurate, to accuse people of faith within their own denominations of being extremists or theocrats when disagreements arise?

Name calling, ad hominem attacks, and a stubborn refusal to participate in dialog have enormous power to hasten irreparable division. The phrase "incompatible with Christianity" appears in belief statements of several denominations. More conservative denominations, like the Assemblies of God denomination, call homosexuality "an aberration, evil, a problem, sin against God and man, ungodly and a perversion. . . . Believers must trust the Holy Spirit to guide them in distinguishing between those [homosexuals] who want God's salvation and those who may be recruiting sympathizers for homosexuality as an alternate life-style."[2] The Mormon Church officially believes that homosexuality is a chosen lifestyle, caused by dysfunctional parenting, and can be cured through therapy and prayer—positions that are in agreement with statements of even liberal religious faith groups. Such positions serve to silence dialog and to tether parishioners and their ministers to positions with which they don't necessarily agree.

But how long can Christians wait, as the debate rages on or festers at the threshold of consciousness, for justice? How long must churches struggle in silence or open conflict before freedom comes?

The Resurrection of Sincerity

In his naïve trust of a world whose nature he did not grasp, gay University of Wyoming student Matthew Shepard might have been anyone's younger brother—but one who had been transformed "into a symbol of rage so immense and inchoate that it was hard to imagine that . . . he had actually been a young man."[3] Because Americans empathized with the young man, many regarded gay and lesbian friends, relatives, and acquaintances with fresh perspective. Gay men and lesbians now presented new challenges for growth within the hearts and minds of their straight Christian brothers and sisters.

In October 1998, Matthew was assaulted, robbed, and left to die, tethered to a deer fence "like a scarecrow." Within five days, he died in a hospital intensive care unit in Laramie, Wyoming without ever regaining consciousness. His parents kept a bedside vigil until the end. Fred Phelps, a fundamentalist minister from Topeka, Kansas, and members of his family stationed themselves across the street from the Episcopal church where Matthew's funeral occurred, carrying signs and shouting slogans of condemnation: "Fags Die, God Laughs," and "No Tears for Queers." Citizens everywhere had no choice but to take a closer look at hatred's potential to incite violence. Many religious leaders were stunned, then outraged.

"The fact that Matthew was an Episcopalian makes our grief no [sharper], but it does give us a particular responsibility to stand with gays and lesbians," said Frank T. Griswold, Presiding Bishop of the Episcopal Church USA, in an official statement. "[It gives us a responsibility] to decry all forms of violence against them—from verbal to physical, and to encourage the dialogue that can, with God's help, lead to new appreciation for their presence in the life of our church, and the broader community."

Mel White, author of *Stranger at the Gate: To Be Gay and Christian in America,* spoke in a weary voice that communicated clearly the effects Matthew Shepard's death had on him. Shepard's murder compelled him to reexamine the responses of faith communities toward gay and lesbian Americans, and he didn't like what he saw.

Mel is angry at the many injustices committed against gay and lesbian Americans, often in the name of Christianity. Through his association with the King Center in Atlanta, Mel studied the philosophies of Mahatma Gandhi, Dr. King's mentor. He even spent time in India with Gandhi's grandson, Arun Gandhi, visiting ashrams and archives, meeting men and women who had actually worked with Gandhi. Mel calls his current mode of fighting against orientation-based bias Soulforce. Based on Gandhi's teachings, Soulforce is a reference to nonviolent "force" that engages one's adversary on a spiritual level.

"Gandhi's system is desperately needed to transform our [gay and lesbian] community," Mel says. "You can't go into Soulforce mode without impacting adversaries. We must say to Pat Robertson, Jerry Falwell, and the others: Sit down with us and negotiate an end to this false rhetoric. If they won't negotiate, then we must take nonviolent direct actions that will move them lovingly in that direction. It is important to find the common ground on which we stand, to negotiate in good faith, to find a third position we both can support. Unfortunately," he adds, "they aren't negotiating an end to their toxic antigay campaign. Therefore, it is time to act."

Often, televangelists who preach against the "abomination" of homosexuality are accused of exploiting homosexuality for the sake of making a buck. And though Mel agrees that they use the fear of homosexuality to raise funds and mobilize volunteers, he is convinced that they are sincere in their beliefs about homosexuality. "They really believe that we are sick and sinful," he explains, "but now they can't even hear the scientific and psychological evidences because they've been using the 'gay threat' so long to raise funds, they've painted themselves into a corner."

Mel is recruiting and training a Network of Soulforce Friends across the country who will join him in direct action to confront and end the antigay rhetoric.

According to Mel, it is not only the television variety of fundamentalism that threatens the delivery of justice to gay and lesbian Americans. "Fundamentalism, on a historic level, is on the loose within mainline denominations," he explains. "Fundamentalism, at its very heart, is orthodoxy gone cultic. It is an urge to purge. Even the mainline churches are doing this purge number. They are searching for 'the wrong kind' of pastors so they can kick them out. There's a kind of hunt going on now for gay and lesbian pastors, and for straight pastors sympathetic to gays and lesbians. And that hunt is coming from the fundamentalist urge to purge."

Mel feels American society has landed in the middle of a major paradigm shift. "The real issue is not homosexuality, but fundamentalism," he explains. "We must help the church understand what kind of thinking is behind this cultic force within Christianity. Faith communities grow more and more exclusive. Inclusive churches are being excluded from the life of their own denominations. We are headed toward a total division—a breach—in the church."

To avoid a controversy that threatens to split congregations, churches must resolve conflicts in revolutionary ways. "Since we have found no solutions to our differences, we need to commit to Gandhi's and King's way of solving problems," Mel continues. "Soulforce is also Jesus' way. We need to love our enemies, and at the same time, to help save them—and us—from their tragic idea. In the process, both sides can change. We need to find a third position. Right now, answers seem to be 'either-or.' But this either-or shift is dangerous. If we don't find another way, the controversy will lead to violence." Mel provides an example of a "third-position" approach. "Marriage is important to the gay community. We are denied the 1,047 rights and protections that go with marriage," he says. "But in Hawaii, they're looking at domestic partnership rights. Maybe by giving up on our right to the word *marriage,* we can gain the right of marriage. Yeah, that's second prize; no one *wants* second prize. But Gandhi cautions us not to predict what the third position might be. Let's work on things we agree on, then compromise on our disagreements. Gandhi's way strikes many as naïve, but what options do we have other than chaos?"

Mel asserts that fundamentalism, by its very nature, assaults and clutches the issues—like same-sex marriage—and "won't let go. Fundamentalists are determined to win—even if winning means winning like the widow who hangs on to the judge's throat until he says, in retreat, 'Okay, okay! I'll free you.' Clinton's impeachment wouldn't have happened without the likes of Gary Bauer and Pat Robertson. They laughed at Mrs. Clinton when she said members of a conspiratorial right wing brought about impeachment. But that's exactly what happened." What's their motivation? "Fundamentalists feel called to make the world right for Jesus to come back. As wonderful as that may sound, the truth is you're a danger to all the rest of us when you have that kind of arrogant zeal. Then, we have the terrible problem in our own community of so many people having been damaged by religion. So we're ready to throw the baby out with the bath. And who can blame gays and lesbians for that? But we are a spiritual community; we're homospiritual and always have been. We have been at the heart of all these religious traditions from the start."

Although ministers in metropolitan areas often call faith communities to embrace gay and lesbian lives through activism and justice making, places like New York City and San Francisco have scant appreciation of the problems faced by gays and lesbians in Middle America, notes Mel. "There is tremendous pressure all across the country on closeted folks who live their lives in terror. The only thing that will survive the threats is faith. Churches must accept homosexuality and spirituality. They must accept the fact that we are homospiritual. Given the chance, we can bring new life to the body of Christ. Yet, at the same time, gay and lesbian people often tell me they don't want to go back to churches that have rejected them. Walt Whitman said to reexamine everything we've been taught, then discard that which insults our souls, and begin again."

That America's youth offer hope for positive change may be a hot topic for the press, but Mel doesn't buy it, not completely. "I don't see that hope when I speak with young people," he says. "Who kills the most gays and lesbians in our country? All the deceptively sophisticated rhetoric of fundamentalism trickles down to baseball bats in the hands of youth. I've walked across many university campuses in this country. Many members of the student body have never taken a stand before; they don't even know what it means to take a stand. I encounter an incredible amount of resistance. All these young people carry signs—young adults who belong to Campus Crusade for Christ, for example, an organization whose members tried to wrest the microphone from my grasp while I spoke on one campus—stating that AIDS is God's punishment for being homosexual. What a nasty, toxic environment many colleges and universities provide for kids!"

Mel faults the closet for perpetuating a climate that cultivates antigay attitudes. "It's still the main place where gay and lesbian people live," Mel says,

"and it is a place of death. Like me, young gay men and women enter heterosexual marriages, hoping their feelings will change. On television, we see gays
and lesbians in Greenwich Village or the Castro, and think: 'Oh, everybody's
all out, and safe and sound.' That's the biggest delusion we have. Those places
are like ghettos. The more I read about the ghettos in Poland, the more I feel
that if they put up fences in places like the Village, we'll have our own ghetto."
Mel pauses, then sighs wearily. "Believe it or not, I'm not an alarmist. Gary and
I have been on the road for six years. We have sat with grassroots organizations in many, many towns. So many gay, lesbian, bisexual, and transgendered
people out there are scared. It's everywhere, this fundamentalist influence."

According to Mel, Matt Shepard's tragic death may have turned many
Americans against such influence. "His death deeply moved the nation," he
says. "He personified what suffering looks like. When America looked up,
they felt something. Predictably, the Religious Right took a little time off to
develop their spin. They said he had been a predator once. Was it one brief,
shining moment that changed minds and hearts? The truth is, many of us may
hang on the stake before minds and hearts are changed in any lasting way."

Lately, too many people have been telling Mel that time is on the side of
justice. "Not true," he says. "You struggle until you win it. Time is never on
the side of justice. It's on the side of injustice. The more we wait, the more
we give away. While we wait, the fundamentalist right is changing the hearts
and minds of the nation. We put out fires, but we don't go after the arsonists.
We must confront what is happening with truth and love, relentlessly. You
see, neither Gandhi nor King had enough time on earth to systematize their
nonviolent method. But they left hundreds of pages of incredible writings on
nonviolence. Now, I'm doing this arrogant, unbelievable thing of trying to
apply it to our cause."

Perhaps it's time, Mel says, for gay and lesbian Christians to stand up and
walk out of the sanctuaries where ministers condemn them for who and how
they love. "Donna Redwing told me about a minister in an African-American
church who blasted gays and lesbians in his sermon," he relates. "His
organist stood up in the middle of church and said, 'There will be no music
today.' And he walked out. We have always been in every faith movement.
When we stay in the closet—when we are silent in the face of abuse and
lies—we are cooperating with evil."

Mel sighs. His ministry has changed directions, and the anxiety and excitement of new challenge are apparent in his voice. He is devoting more
time to studying Gandhi's teachings and to writing a Soulforce sequel to
Stranger at the Gate. The sequel would be a handbook for putting Gandhi's
principles to work. "Gandhi knew about Jesus," he says quietly. "He turned
Jesus' principles into practice and changed two countries. King took up the
banner and helped change a third. Perhaps, with Gandhi's and King's approach, we could transform and renew our own movement."

It's Like the Titanic

The controversy surrounding the union of Jeanne Barnett, 68, and her partner of fifteen years, Ellie Charlton, 63, blessed in January 1999 by ninety-four United Methodist ministers in Sacramento, California, would never have occurred without the highly publicized precedent of Jimmy Creech, who officiated at a September 1997 holy union ceremony for two lesbian members of his Omaha, Nebraska, church. Since then, a number of conservative United Methodist ministers have threatened to leave their parishes rather than fight what they consider to be an increasingly liberal church bureaucracy. "[The United Methodist Church] is like the Titanic," said Andrew Vom Steege, pastor of St. Luke United Methodist Church in Richmond, California, who feels UMC should demand a more traditional hermeneutic about human sexuality (*Los Angeles Times,* May 9, 1998). "It's a sinking ship."

On January 26, 1998, Creech submitted his formal response to the judicial charge that the same-sex holy union ceremony he performed was in disobedience to the Order and Discipline of the United Methodist Church. "I welcome the trial as an opportunity to both make my case and to challenge the unjust position of the UMC regarding lesbians and gay men," Creech wrote. "It is my hope that when the final verdict has been determined, the Social Principles will be affirmed as 'advisory and persuasive' and that there will be greater openness, acceptance, and justice for gay men and lesbians in the United Methodist Church. I contend that I have not acted in disobedience to the Order and Discipline of the UMC, but, after 'prayerful, studied dialogue of faith and practice,' have acted in a way consistent with the gospel of Jesus Christ and with my calling as a pastor."[4]

By a slim margin—eight jurors voted against Creech, but a conviction required nine votes—he was acquitted of charges of disobedience, thereby remaining a pastor in good standing within the United Methodist Church. Despite his exoneration, however, his bishop blocked his return to his church. The bishop presented two options: to be reassigned or to take a sabbatical.

Creech chose the sabbatical. With his wife, he returned to North Carolina, his home state, where they cleaned apartments for a while to make ends meet. By the end of the summer, the Creech family moved to Raleigh. Meanwhile, in one forum after another, Creech stood by his conviction that "to be gay is in itself healthy, normal and natural"—a point of view that ruffled the feathers of some parishioners in Nebraska who left Omaha's First United Methodist Church to start a church of their own. (In late 1998, the UMC officially recognized the "rogue group" as a mission church.)

Once the trial repercussions subsided, several conservative UMC groups requested enforceable prohibitions against same-sex ceremonies; in fact, these groups demanded a special 1998 session of the General Conference, even though the next Conference session was not scheduled until 2000. But the bishops denied the request. "The intensity of this issue [homosexuality] is greater than any I have seen in my forty years of ministry," said Bishop George Bashore, president of the UMC Council of Bishops.[5] "The potential for schism and hemorrhaging is greater now than at any time I have ever seen in the life of the church."

Then, in August 1998, the UMC Judicial Council, the denomination's highest court, ruled that the prohibition against performing same-sex ceremonies was binding. Pastors who performed such ceremonies could be defrocked. "That decision is an act of institutional violence," Creech said during a lecture in Pittsburgh (September 13, 1998).

However, the issue of same-sex commitment ceremonies—and whether UMC ministers would be allowed to officiate—promised to be resurrected when the UMC ushered in the new millenium at its next conference in Cleveland, Ohio. "This [issue] has been with us a long time and will not go away," said Ron Hodges, pastor of Christ United Methodist Church in Salt Lake City (*Salt Lake Tribune,* November 21, 1998). "But I think there will come a time when we look back and say . . . there are many similarities between this and the civil rights issues of the 1960s." In fact, a century passed before Methodists began to mend their Civil War-era rift over slavery. Acceptance of women clergy was also agonizingly delayed.

By October 11, 1998, three hundred sixty three United Methodist ministers had signed an open letter, sent to the bishops of the United Methodist Church, urging them to "move beyond [the] silence and inaction" they had previously taken toward the Methodist prohibition against the celebration of gay and lesbian unions. The letter implored the bishops to initiate a massive education campaign in the UMC "so that misunderstandings about the nature of scriptural authority can be addressed" and members can learn "how a noncondemning acceptance of homosexuality is a legitimate position within our Wesleyan tradition. These are dark days for our church and for those who seek to embody the prophetic justice of our Christian tradition," the letter stated. "Our church is adrift, buffeted by forces that seek to steer our course away from the prophetic, just, and compassionate course of Christ. Our church is inundated with a cacophony of voices that seek to make literal the writings of John Wesley, and use them as weapons, even as they do the same with the living witness of our scripture. We will become a denomination of 'winners' and 'losers,' where authority will be determined by the judgment of ecclesiastical trial."

UMC leadership was completely aware of the possibility of schism, as evidenced by the February 1998 completion of a document called "In Search of Unity." Because "some persons suggest that a split could occur because of the depth of the conflict and the disturbing choices people feel compelled to make," according to Bruce W. Robbins, General Secretary, General Commission on Christian Unity and Interreligious Concerns, "[we call for] a conversation between more liberal and more conservative voices within the United Methodist Church." The document acknowledged two distinct but opposing fronts within the denomination. "Those who see no barrier to full admission of homosexuals who are morally responsible and committed Christians to the church's orders and rites believe this to be consistent with Christian teaching, or required by the love and compassion expressed by Christ," it states. "Those who oppose the admission of homosexuals to the Church's orders and rites believe that such a proposed practice is inconsistent with Christian teaching. Within each of these groups—compatibilists and incompatibilists—we can identify people representing perspectives which are both 'more liberal' and 'more conservative.' Compatibilists believe that the failure to include homosexual persons in the full life of the church, including ordination, means the exclusion of many faithful members who have been for much too long oppressed by the limited interpretation of traditional church teaching and practices. For these compatibilists, liberation of the oppressed is a sign of the coming of God's rule."

The same month, some Methodists called for an end to the persistent debate over sexual orientation issues. "We're all weary of being preoccupied with the issue of homosexuality, but that is the issue the church is preoccupied with, and to ignore that is to ignore what is going on out there," said Rev. Maxie Dunnam, president of Asbury Theological Seminary in Wilmore, Kentucky (United Methodist News Service, February 1998).

But no one could ignore the more than twelve hundred well-wishers who attended the union of the lesbian couple in California, nor the scores of ministers who acted in defiance of the UMC law forbidding them from performing "ceremonies that celebrate homosexual unions." As the service began, about five hundred religious and civil rights activists clasped hands and bowed their heads in prayer. "If anybody wants to file charges against us," said Don Fado, the couple's pastor, to the *Sacramento Bee* (January 17, 1999), "this is what the charges are for: praying this prayer." The prayer was an appeal to "God, our creator . . . to guide, strengthen, and keep Jeanne and Ellie open to your spirit."

However, Fado would not be the only minister to face the music. Ninety-four other pastors, as well as seventy-one clergy members who lent their names in absentia, could lose their clerical jobs. United Methodist Bishop Melvin Talbert announced January 21, 1999, that UMC officials would investigate the holy union in order to decide whether to file a complaint (*Fresno Bee,* January 23, 1999)—a decision that Fado said was an appropriate one. "There is no debate that we violated church rules," he said. "The question is how serious an offense the church considers this to be and what is the appropriate reaction of the church when people in good conscience obey the call of Christ as they understand it."

In March 1999, Bishop Melvin Talbert "reluctantly" filed formal complaints against sixty-nine pastors who took part in the Sacramento service.[6] Bishop Talbert, who does not support the UMC ban against same-sex unions, said he would rather draw "the circle of full membership to include homosexuals without judgment."

The Pain of Separation

Faith communities increasingly face the prospect of dramatic change within their denominations. Regardless of their response to gay and lesbian issues— whether more conciliatory or more aligned with conservative biblical interpretation—anxiety increases. Homosexuality as a religious topic allows little room for vacillation or neutrality. At times, parishioners perceive defection as their only choice when church policies are altered in ways incompatible with their lives of faith. Standing firmly by their commitments to either progressive or conservative views of inclusion, ordination, and same-sex holy-union issues, parishioners frequently react with skepticism when their church leaders reassure them that their denominations will escape schism. To many, the question is not whether schism will occur, but when. Two important questions weigh on the Christian conscience. Does schism constitute the worst consequence to communities of faith? Or do believers accept schism as part of Christianity's evolution?

"The question is, who walks?"

Mark Silk, Director of the Center for the Study of Religion in Public Life at Trinity College in Hartford, Connecticut, posed this question to Mark I. Pinsky, writing for *The Orlando Sentinel* (December 4, 1998). "People have always 'walked' in American religion. The gay issue is the real third rail out there. That's what's sending the sparks flying." The gay and lesbian issue, Silk says, will be "an ongoing struggle in religion because [it] is an ongoing struggle in American life."

In the Roman Catholic Church, despite recent attempts to reach out to gay and lesbian worshipers, including the establishment of special target ministries, Rev. John Harvey called on fellow Roman Catholics to join him "in a battle [against] the gay movement." He called his proposed fight against homosexuality a part "of a cultural war between Christianity and radical liberalism."[7]

The Presbyterian Church (U.S.A.) began its third decade of arguing over whether to ordain gay men and women to the ministry. To some, the argument seemed moot. Pamela Byers, director of Covenant Network of Presbyterians, a national organization that supports an official opening of the ministry to gays and lesbians, estimates that hundreds, if not thousands, of current Presbyterian ministers, though gay and lesbian, already serve congregations—and serve them effectively (*Denver Post,* October 25, 1998).

In Marlborough, Massachusetts, Holy Trinity Episcopal Church decided to couple talk with action. Because of the church's perception that the ECUSA betrayed its commitment to biblical standards in its increasingly receptive stance toward gay and lesbian inclusion, the sixty-member parish voted to withhold its annual diocesan assessment of almost two thousand dollars (*Boston Globe,* December 20, 1998). Judith Gentle-Hardy, Holy Trinity's rector, informed the leader of the Episcopal Diocese of Massachusetts that she no longer recognized his authority.

Gentle-Hardy recognized that her action could force the diocese to re-move her and take control of the church's real estate. "Our position [is] that homosexuality is against God's will," she explained. "Those who find them-selves in homosexual bondage are welcome to come to our church and ex-perience the healing power of Jesus Christ."

Gentle-Hardy said her church's decision was "buoyed" by the Canterbury resolution, a strict statement against inclusive ordination and same-sex union policies that passed during the Lambeth Conference in England. Episco-palians United, a conservative organization within ECUSA, warned that "whoever pressures the church to alter the normativeness of its teaching with regard to homosexuality must be aware that that person promotes schism in the church." But Bishop George Hunt, in his 1995 farewell address to the Diocese of Rhode Island, asserted that "there can be no real unity when jus-tice is postponed. . . . If this means that some in conscience must leave this fold, then we must bid them Godspeed and offer our prayers for them as they continue to follow what they believe to be God's will. Our own course is clear. In this diocese, it is our policy to follow the Canons of General Con-vention. Simply, this means that all people, whatever their gender, whatever their orientation sexually, are eligible for consideration and calling to ordi-nation and to every ordained position."[8]

Hunt had only one response to those Episcopalians lamenting that the de-nomination was moving too fast toward acceptance of gay and lesbian lives on equal footing with heterosexual lives. "Justice in this matter has been post-poned for almost two thousand years," he said.

Central Florida Bishop John W. Howe told the *Central Florida Episco-palian* (July 1997) that the Episcopal Church had reneged on its promise neither to develop nor use "blessings of same-sex unions." "Two conclu-sions are beyond dispute," Bishop Howe said. "The traditional, biblical understanding of sexual morality which is so widely caricatured by some within the American Church as 'extreme' and 'marginal' is actually the essence of historic mainstream Anglican Christianity. And, if the Episco-pal Church continues in its present direction, we can see it being margin-alized by the rest of the Communion, and perhaps the wide ecumenical Church, in rather short order. Bottom line? In the name of 'homosexual rights,' an agenda is being pressed by some that threatens schism within the Episcopal Church, and ostracism within the Anglican Communion and beyond."

The Lambeth Conference delivered the biggest blow thus far against the shift of the Episcopal Church USA toward gay and lesbian inclusion. During its July/August 1998 conference, a committee studying sexuality issues de-nounced American churches perceived as having compromised in their views of homosexuality. Before Lambeth began, Bishop John Shelby Spong had char-acterized conservatives within the ECUSA as "uninformed religious people" whose literal interpretation of the Bible "has become one of embarrassment to the cause of Christ." But some conservatives feared that if the ordination of homosexual priests and the blessing of same-sex unions "get their noses under the door, [they] will become mandatory in time, as well."[9] Spong considered the conservative stance impulsive. He said bishops wanted to establish more tolerance, not conformity of all churches to one position. "They are not facing my reality," Spong said. "I've got up to thirty gay priests in my diocese who are absolutely magnificent. I would have to close up our urban ministry if I didn't have gay priests because I can't get a heterosexual couple to live in some of our ghettos." When other priests cautioned that the direction of the ECUSA might cause schism, Spong expressed little concern. "I am not interested in being a member of a racist church, a chauvinist church, or a homophobic church," he said. "If the price of being truthful is a division in the church, so be it. That doesn't worry me at all. God's truth will win out."

Besides, Lambeth's consideration of homosexuality as sin holds scarce legislative value to the Episcopal Church. "As an educated priest, I'm not bound by what Lambeth does," says Jim V. Bills, vicar of St. Stephen's Episcopal Church in Charleston, South Carolina. Jim is a married, heterosexual minister whose previous parish experience in Tennessee compelled him to reexamine his attitudes toward gays and lesbians. Sharing in the lives of gay and lesbian Christians, he says, allowed him to become a "whole priest." "Lambeth is a political football, basically. The frustrating piece is that Lambeth spoke, and its words are being seized by the conservative element. Some say this is what the bishops of the world believe. But it's simply not true. The Episcopal Church USA is an autonomously governed entity. I'm here, and I will never change who I am, no matter what. I'm old enough that I no longer have to be successful; I can be faithful instead—and that's more fun."

In an unlikely turn of events, considering the typical Southern Baptist stance toward homosexuality, parishioners at Wake Forest Baptist Church cleared the way for their ministers to perform gay and lesbian unions (*News & Observer,* November 16, 1998), but stopped short of formally endorsing these unions. Instead, the church issued a resolution that "only God can bless relationships between two people." Still, the church faces almost certain expulsion from the Baptist State Convention of North Carolina. According to Convention President Mac Brunson, "We [don't] condone sin."

Despite the likely expulsion, members of Wake Forest Baptist Church considered the relationships among their church members far more important to them than membership in the state Convention. "We are at a time when increasing fragmentation is taking place in the old Baptist system," said Bill Leonard, dean of the Divinity School at Wake Forest University. "There seems to be more questioning of official ties to the Southern Baptist Convention."

Wake Forest wasn't the first Baptist congregation on the front lines embroiled in battles with state and regional associations. Larry Bethune, pastor of University Baptist Church in Austin, Texas, learned via a message left on his answering machine that the Baptist General Convention of Texas (BGCT) had voted on January 30, 1998, to "distance" itself from his church because of its policies of inclusion toward its gay and lesbian members. "The church supports a practice that Baptists in Texas consider to be in conflict with spiritual guidelines," wrote Charles Davenport, chairman of the Administrative Committee of the BGCT's Executive Board.[10] "Information published by the church clearly indicates approval of homosexual practice. . . . We commend those churches who seek to minister to those persons who engage in homosexual behavior. We cannot, however, approve of churches' endorsing homosexual practice as biblically legitimate."

Circumstances leading to the rift began in 1994, when the church ordained Hans Venable, an openly gay deacon. In protest, about one hundred parishioners eventually left the congregation. Since then, the church population has exceeded its original membership and is still growing. Larry says his gay and lesbian parishioners "have modeled the love of Christ. They are giving their lives here alongside the rest of us, evidencing the signs of God's Spirit in their lives. They are our brothers and sisters, and we will not abandon them because of outside pressure. It's no big deal; we're simply doing the right thing."

Larry admits that his church lost a "good partnership in some important mission work." But in matters of relational orientation, "Texas Baptists have done damage. I am a white, male, heterosexual, middle-class American, and kind of a big guy at that," he says. "I am a member of the most privileged and powerful group in history. But now, I have been on the receiving end of prejudice. We have been marginalized for standing with the marginalized, and it is good for our souls to get a small taste of what people of color, and women, and our gay and lesbian friends and their families face every day of their lives."

Larry never considered issues of homosexuality—at least in any substantive way—until the controversy over Hans Venable's ordination began. "I had to follow where my conscience led," he says. "I'm not an expert on sexuality or on human physiology. I received my doctorate in Old and New Testament studies. I just didn't see anything in scripture that was so condemning of homosexual persons. The Bible doesn't know anything about orientation as we see it today. Certainly, it does prohibit certain homosexual behaviors, like rape, pederasty, and prostitution. Beyond those prohibitions, the Bible is silent."

Larry's contemplation and study of the issues are reflected in the continuing growth of his congregation—of both orientations. Of his current three hundred parishioners, about sixty of them are gay and lesbian. "We have a great, wonderful mix of seniors, heterosexual singles, blacks and whites, heterosexual married couples, and of course, our gay and lesbian members," he continues. "That's the kind of diversity we like. And here's a beautiful thing.

We started out talking about ministering *to* gays and lesbians. Now, we speak of ministering *with* them. We realized how much our lives had gained spiritually from being inclusive—from hearing their stories, sharing their giftedness, and standing with them."

Despite the growth of University Baptist Church, Larry is convinced that gay and lesbian issues will "divide the church the way slavery did, only without the geographical division. But I will not change my mind, because I believe in the truth of this issue. The majority of Christians will come around to it. It may take one hundred fifty years—and Lord knows what—but I believe the truth belongs to God."

Meanwhile, University Baptist Church has continued its journey in ministering with gay and lesbian Christians. "Our deacons established a group that led the church to reflect upon the meaning of covenant partnerships," he relates. "I asked them if they would give me permission to have gay union services in our sanctuary. We decided to study it carefully, rather than assuming that's where we had to go on our journey. That study also led us to determine more accurately what heterosexual marriage means." In March 1999, the church approved a new Christian wedding policy that includes homosexual unions and requires all couples contemplating covenant partnership to receive at least six hours of premarital preparation.

A Schism of Self

Father Warren Gress doubts that the Roman Catholic Church will experience schism similar to mainline Protestant denominations. However, like Protestantism, Catholicism's response to homosexual issues creates conflicts on both personal and organizational levels, and forces ministers and parishioners to choose between church doctrine and their conscience.

During thirteen years as a parish priest, the duplicity of being publicly single and privately partnered tore Warren apart. "I could see myself with Jim, I could see myself making a public commitment to him," Warren says. "Every once in a while, we would talk about that possibility."

After five years of therapy, Warren agreed to a commitment ceremony.

"We did it, finally, and invited members of my family, and friends, and people from my parish," Warren recalls. "The ceremony was performed in an Episcopal church. Afterwards, I knew my ministry was not long in this world. But what that ceremony made me realize was that for ten years, my primary commitment had been to Jim. Don't get me wrong. I loved the ministry. I was good at it. Yet I knew that if the Bishop ever called me in, and I was forced to make a choice, I would choose Jim."

Warren gave himself a year to determine whether he really wanted to leave the priesthood. "After six months, I was sure."

Looking back, Warren feels that full acknowledgment of his sexual orientation—an acknowledgment manifested through his love for Jim—

made him a more effective priest. "I found that when I was honest about my sexuality, I was more honest in my prayer," he explains. "When I worked with gay and lesbian people, I asked: Do you bring your sexuality to your prayer? It's who we are. That's the big hurdle we need to clear—to be able to thank God for who we are. It was a big hurdle for me to say, God, thank You for who I am. But that's a most important place to be."

How could a man who loved the priesthood so much finally give it up? "Many of my acquaintances in the priesthood say they just ignore it—this alienation, this schism, this splintering of one's life," he explains. "I spent so much energy keeping parts of my life at a distance from one another! If I tried to live as just a priest—or just a man in a relationship—my life would never have come together the way it has now. I had to ask myself a number of questions. What was really life-giving? What was the background music that kept me going? It was—and is—my relationship with Jim. Even as a priest, I had to start moving in that direction. The choice had to be made. One part of my life strongly affirmed who I was as a gay person, while the other affirmed my talents and capabilities. But I finally realized that I didn't have to be a priest to be a believer. God would still love me, even if I wasn't a priest anymore."

Now, Warren's ministry is partially defined by his role as youth coordinator for WeAreFamily, a Charleston-based organization whose mission is to "encourage straight and gay/lesbian members of our community to value one another through education." Though he has left the Roman Catholic Church, Warren serves on the administrative staff of St. Stephen Episcopal Church in Charleston. Occasionally, he leads Sunday service. Warren perceives his ministry to entail taking advantage of opportunities to show heterosexuals that there are few differences between them and their gay and lesbian acquaintances. "The more we can present images of [gay and lesbian] people 'just like you,' the better," he says. "One basic difference between me and my straight friends is the way I genitally express my affection for another person. By and large, my life is just as ordinary as anyone else's. The more people see and discover that, the better for all of us."

Warren recently chose to join the Episcopal Church. "I can see a split coming [in the Episcopal Church]," he says. "This is a church with a weaker move toward a central teaching ministry." In the Roman Catholic Church, current thinking leans toward natural law and a more conservative scriptural understanding of human sexuality. "The Episcopal Church has a much greater focus on local church rules and practices—unlike Catholicism. The split could easily become one between the Western churches and those of Africa and the East. It could also be seen as an attempt to form a more fundamental, scripturally based church community—a reform that is not far off the horizon."

Warren believes that, in most faith communities, homosexuality will remain a highly charged issue into the foreseeable future. "Many people will continue to struggle with their comfort levels," he explains. "But I will work within a church that welcomes gay and lesbian persons, or is at least on the journey toward that moment. My calling to minister to the people God gathers is to minister as a gay person—not as a closeted Catholic priest. My sexuality cannot be divorced from who I am. For me to minister to the people of God without acknowledging this fundamental aspect of my identity is to minister as a fragmented person. And I have had enough of that."

A Time for Discernment

Ordained a Presbyterian minister in 1982, Lee Gibson, a "parish associate" in a New Mexico parish, began consideration of the ministry when he was only twelve years old. However, the actual process began in 1978, "when the Presbyterians started with the first task force on homosexuality. At the time I was a senior in a conservative evangelical college. Although I realized my attraction to men, I understood I would have to fight to overcome it."

And he fought it "like hell—until I was out of the seminary. When I was ordained, I was still fighting it. Finally, I acknowledged my sexual orientation—at least, to myself. For a while, I thought I would dry up inside and just blow away."

Ultimately, Lee's understanding of God's purpose for human sexuality nudged him toward a positive self-image. "One of the things I've always loved about the Protestant tradition is the elevation it gives to relational sexuality," he explains. "My partner and I have been together for twelve years. He and I have a deeply committed relationship."

Once Lee assumed a prominent role as parish associate, only one or two parishioners withdrew from their small church. "Most of our parishioners like us and accept us. Theologically, however, a couple of them have a difficult time affirming us as a couple in leadership roles. But the personal relationship we have with them takes precedence over their beliefs." As an example, Lee tells of one parishioner who was convinced all gay men were pedophiles. "She just couldn't get it through her head the fallacy of that belief," Lee says. "It was a long-time assumption that was difficult for her to overcome. But she really likes us, and we've blown away that stereotype. I discovered part of her problem. For a long time, New Mexico was the 'dumping ground' for pedophile [Roman Catholic] priests who were sent to local facilities for treatment. Lots of those priests were assimilated into the local diocese."

Only through personal relationships with gay and lesbian people are straight Christians able to rethink their positions about homosexuality, Lee says. "Ideological head-to-head is very difficult. A conservative college professor of mine visited with us while he and his wife were traveling in the area. He questioned me about why I thought I was entitled to retain my ordination—both from a biblical and theological perspective. Well, I explained my biblical and theological rationale in depth. Afterwards, he conceded that what I said sounded as though it landed in the parameters of the Reformed tradition. In the Presbyterian Church," Lee adds, "it helps to have a well-developed hermeneutical stance that you can articulate well."

Before moving to New Mexico, Lee was always very cautious not to affirm his orientation. "I was never officially out," he explains. "I never said the words 'I'm gay' to the congregation. Even now, I play my cards very close to my vest in the wider church. When I preached in Chicago, the whole Janie Spahr [see Chapter 3] thing hit the Presbyterian Church. At the time, there was a tacit don't-ask-don't-tell understanding, and officials in the presbytery knew I was gay. But when the shit hits the fan, presbytery leaders must stick to policy. At one point, I refused to set foot in a church for two years. I felt that outraged—that hurt."

The fact that gay and lesbian ministers cannot safely affirm their identities in fullness within the Presbyterian Church, Lee says, is contrary to what church is all about—and is part of the current anxiety about the possibility of schism. "As parishioners and their ministers share their stories, their churches are formed," he reasons. "A church has the responsibility to live together in love and understanding. As Christians, we should pray to find that love, that understanding. That's the most dangerous prayer we can pray. When we pray, we have no choice but to adapt and change. That's what prayer is all about. If it is God's will that 10 percent of creation is gay, then how can a person be at peace if he or she lives outside God's will? I think most people, straight or gay, believe that each person exists as God intends that person to be. There's no 'better' person; there's no 'worse' person. Straight isn't better than gay, nor gay better than straight. There's just difference and diversity. Homosexuality is part of the diversity that God has built into the system."

Because of the General Assembly's majority disregard of God's system of diversity, the Presbyterian Church is treading on "very shaky theological ground," Lee asserts. "Resulting from the change of constitutional standards within the Presbyterian Church (U.S.A.)," Lee says, "more and more of us [ministers] are beginning to question our roles. I'd rather we started a new Presbyterian Church. I think we have to have some wise discernment on what to do at this point. Gay and lesbian people are clearly called to God's ministry. What, in obedience to God, are we supposed to do about that? Yes, homosexuality looks like a red flag issue in our church, but there are really two gospels at war in all mainline traditions. It's the war of the right-wing gospel versus the gospel of inclusiveness and diversity. We're still in process. We have yet to see how these two gospels are going to deal with it. Will they fight it out? Or will they learn to coexist?"

Still, Lee isn't convinced that schism will occur within the PC(USA). "If so, sexual orientation will be just one of the fracturing elements," he explains.

"There's a big split over the whole meaning of the gospel itself. Besides, the whole concept of denominationalism may be a dinosaur. Denominational structures are close to imploding in the face of increasing financial straits and aging constituencies. The so-called 'culture wars' are more a squabbling over why we're dying and who gets the bank accounts."

Lee thinks, in some ways, that the deconstruction of Christianity will allow "new forms and expressions that are more synchronous with our era to arise. That's what happened in the Reformation and may be poised to happen again. No one can predict. But if schism occurs, I hope to find a place to preserve my ordination credentials in the new, emerging patterns. My 'call to ministry' is not tied to structure; it's a response to God. I'll keep ministering in some way."

Shaking Hands with Clenched Fists

Years ago, my "practice" of Christianity brought about a sense of fullness in identity. In fact, nowhere did I feel as completely affirmed as a human being as I did in church. No other experience in my life brought me closer to people and to God like my experience of being a Christian. Then, homosexuality grew into a controversy of faith—*my* controversy of faith. I became a "marginalized Christian."

Although I felt "other" in most circumstances, I had been "as one" within my faith community. For many years, I thought of Jesus as a maverick, a revolutionary, an innovator. He was the pattern for my life. He was a savior personal enough that I could speak to him in prayer and tap into the strength I gleaned from our conversation to move forward—always forward—in life. Now, because I am part of "the controversy," I often feel betrayed by the same religion that once gave my life meaning. But most of all, I experience sadness and anger—the way a surgery patient might feel after he discovers he's gone under the knife unnecessarily.

On Christmas Eve 1998, after an absence of more than five years, I attended the church of my childhood. The acceptance I once felt at St. Paul had evaporated—not because I was treated any differently than I had been treated in the past. However, because of the policies of exclusion coming from the ELCA, I had become a stranger. When I choked on the words of the liturgy in the *Lutheran Service Book and Hymnal,* I was not overwhelmed by nostalgia or even by a deep sense of reverence. My eyes filled with tears because the words made me feel neither a welcome guest nor a child of God. In fact, they were, now, just words.

During the candlelight portion of the service, the congregation bellowed "Joy to the World." Naturally, I went through the motions. But I considered raising a cold, unlit candle above my head during the final refrain. Although I got cold feet yet again, my partner tapped into a source of courage I did not have. He dropped a note, along with his offering, into the offering plate. His note encouraged the church to maintain dialog on the subject of inclusiveness—a dialog, I later learned from a friend who attends St. Paul, that has never really begun. Unfortunately, the dialog has not begun in many, many churches throughout the country. The laws of silence are pervasive and strong.

How could I find it in my heart to pledge myself to this faith, the way I had once pledged? How could any of us—gay and lesbian Christians, and straight allies in the fight with us—take that leap? We had become what Spong calls "believers in exile."[11]

Rembert Truluck (Chapter2), a Baptist minister-in-exile, feels it may be too late to save most denominations from schism. "I suddenly realized that we, as gay and lesbian people, do not really have to be so afraid of the churches," he says. "Many churches are destroying themselves. Homosexuals were part of the human race long before any churches existed, and we will still be around when all of the present culture, including the churches, are ancient history. Being in the midst of a dead church"—that is, the Southern Baptist Convention—"made me realize how self-destructive most churches are."

When churches identify themselves by people who are not welcome, Rembert says, they cease to be Christian. "Whenever the church devotes its energy to judging and rejecting people and uses its power to exclude people who are different and misunderstood, Jesus walks out and goes home," Rembert says. "Our world is changing. Nobody can stop the changes. We will move into the next century, whether we want to or not, whether we understand what is happening or not. Old axioms and customs are crumbling. New views of reality and of people are emerging. We can be part of the positive and constructive changes that respect every individual as having equal value. We can also be part of the fierce war against human progress and call it 'the will of God,' but calling negative attitudes and abusive religion 'the word of God' or 'the will of God' will not make it so. Sick religion is destructive and deadly, no matter what kind of perfumed and gilded paper is used to wrap it or how many television and radio stations broadcast it every day."

The ministers who reported their experiences from the front realize that most faith communities face divisive battles over sexual orientation issues. Not all, however, feel schism is imminent within their own particular traditions.

Many Roman Catholics feel that a schism has already occurred in their tradition, according to Father Jim Morris (Chapter 2). In October 1986, Cardinal Josef Ratzinger, the Vatican secretary for the Congregation for the Doctrine of the Faith, published a "Letter to the Catholic Bishops on the Pastoral Care of Homosexual Persons." The letter stated that "although the particular inclination of the homosexual person is not a sin, it is a more or less strong tendency ordered toward an intrinsic moral evil; and thus, the inclination itself must be seen as an objective disorder." It was further stated that "all support should be withdrawn from [all] organizations which seek to undermine the teaching of the Church, which are ambiguous about it, or which neglect it entirely. . . . Special attention should be given to the practice of scheduling religious services and the use of Church buildings by these groups."

Within one year's time, "virtually all of the chapters of Dignity had been expelled from Catholic property by their local bishops," Jim continues. "To this date, none have been invited to return. So is Dignity then 'schismatic' or simply [existing] in forced 'exile'? I'm not even sure I know the difference!

"What I do know, however, is that all of the members of Dignity consider themselves to be very much 'Catholic,' the Congregation for the Doctrine of the Faith notwithstanding," Jim continues. "And I also know that many United States bishops have expressed regret, even embarrassment, over Cardinal Ratzinger's definitions and directives."

Jim feels fortunate, even blessed, to be a gay person and a Roman Catholic priest "in this particular time in history." However, Jim rejects the idea that schism has already occurred. Instead, he interprets the current crisis within Catholicism more positively. "Much may be attributed to God and the benevolent workings of God's Holy Spirit," he explains. "The sharp decline in church attendance, in financial contributions, and in vocations to the priesthood and religious life may simply set the stage for an entirely new church in the next millenium. As Rome has become more and more restrictive, the people of God may be remaining respectful and loving, but more discriminating in their hearing.

"There is, I believe then, a new church ahead for all of us. To paraphrase Saint Paul, it is a church where women and men can share their gifts equally, no matter what their state in life or sexual orientation," Jim continues. "It is a church founded upon love, built up by human suffering and sustained by our quest for hope and eternal life in Christ. It is a church that all of us are given the responsibility for creating."

In such a church, Jim asserts, there can be no room for schism. "There is only room for more and more freedom. This church is the reign of God. And we, as Catholics, and therefore as the church, must help this church to happen."

Not all clergy share Jim's cautious optimism about their faith traditions. Not only has the stage been set, but schism has already occurred in the ELCA, according to Rev. Keith Robinson (Chapter 3). "Several pastors have been 'tried' and defrocked for their violation of the church's regulation over their right to be 'practicing homosexuals,'" he says. "Several congregations have left the ELCA as a result."

In California, the pastor of San Marcos Lutheran Church resigned after coming out to his congregation. "In November 1998, several of his followers opened All Saints Lutheran Church, calling him as pastor in open defiance of ELCA practices," Keith relates. "The new congregation—Lutheran by doctrine—is not a member of the ELCA, but it took with it about 75 percent of the members from the previous parish. This new congregation and others in similar situations, or congregations that have left the ELCA over the issue, are now in structured dialog [with each other]. Discussions include the formation of a separate synod, not along geographical lines, but along the lines of openness to gay and lesbian clergy."

In Keith's opinion, these incidents constitute an already-occurring schism within the ELCA, an institution not receptive to change on the subject of homosexuality. "It is thought that there will be one more effort at the ELCA's national assembly in Denver this year (1999) to revise the expectations of the conservative code of ethical standards governing the behavior of clergy," Keith continues. "Written by neoconservatives and affirmed by a political, self-selected assembly delegate system, it is unlikely this document will be overturned. If it is not, divisions within the church will deepen even further."

These assemblies tend to elect available leaders within the local parish structures, leaders who are generally white, conservative, and in late middle age. Lutheran ministers with more progressive voices are largely overlooked. "As long as there is brokenness within the church leadership over the issue, which there clearly is within the ELCA, schism is reality," Keith explains. "Several clergy have already given up their careers, for they have been victims of an internal legal process that, because of separation of church and state laws in this country, discriminates against its employees based on sexual orientation. Its unfair labor practices only add to the brokenness within the churches around gay and lesbian issues."

Keith regards Christianity as a religion filled with diversities. "Christian freedom throughout the ages has given its adherents the right to be different in various cultural settings," he explains. "I see the 'gay issue' as one more such moment in postmodern times that adherents to the faith are struggling with. Some people are walking; some people are supporting an unjust church; some are struggling against the current structures. As it has been, so it will be for the next twenty-five to forty years. Future historians will look back in dismay at the injustices practiced and the scripture abused to advance a neoconservative, moralistic political agenda. Christianity will be enriched only as those who struggle for their God-given rights and their God-given identity grapple with new faith constructs that take the Christian faith to 10 percent of the people who, for centuries, have been denied access to the altar and fellowship of the Body of Christ. Nationwide support systems within and outside of the church, which embody the spirit of Christ and Christ's love, are being established, bringing the gospel in new and creative ways to persons within the gay and lesbian communities."

Each day, Keith prays for strength to continue the ministry to which he has been called. "Each day, I pray for my brothers and sisters who have been clerical martyrs in this battle," he says. "Each day, I must dedicate myself to their support, to more effective ministries within the gay and lesbian community, and to the change of unjust policies in an institution dedicated to the gospel."

As a Christian activist, Keith's dedication to ministry means even more. "I must seek support and I must give support to those clergy struggling with the issue," he explains. "It also means living defensively in a hostile environment. Gay and lesbian pastors with no political experience, with no sense of struggle—just deep personal convictions—must learn how to fight politically. Ecclesial structures carry contemporary political agendas. So it has been throughout the ages. Current ecclesial bodies are deeply impacted in America by neoconservative and conservative moral agendas—homophobia being only one of them. Clergy must understand that the religious struggle for freedom also includes confrontation with a political agenda that means not only death for gays and lesbians, but for minorities, poor persons, women's rights, youth, and persons in developing nations. I work to make the connections so that we can create broad-based political-ecclesial coalitions working for human rights on a number of fronts, including gay and lesbian rights within the churches, even for its clergy."

Nor does the schism controversy spare the MCC tradition. Leslie Addison (Chapter 4), associate pastor of MCC of Greater Hayward in San Lorenzo, California, admits that the word *schism* is emotionally charged. "Do I think that the issue of how mainline denominations respond to gay and lesbian inclusion in the life of the church, including the blessing of relationships without regard to the gender of the people involved, is going to create something as dramatic and separate as eastern orthodoxy, or even Anglicanism?" she asks. "No. Am I confident that churches will gain and lose members because of the stance they take, that clergy will be defrocked, pushed out, or resign? Yes. Why? Because it is what I see happening. I would not be altogether shocked if the issues of sexual orientation do, in fact, cause some splits at the end of this century that are similar to the ones caused by issues of slavery in the middle of the last century. It would be no coincidence that churches who left the parent Presbyterian or Methodist denominations in order to support the subjugation of African Americans might leave again in order to deny the full created-in-the-image-of-God humanity of gays and lesbians."

Will schism in mainline denominations have any significant impact on MCC? "Our church will need to find ways to provide comfort to those who cannot find a safe haven in mainline denominations," Leslie answers. "I expect that issues of sexual orientation will remain on the radar and in the media. I expect that schism will also be accompanied by antigay violence and antigay legislative attempts. At the same time, people of faith who have attempted to be conciliatory and inclusive of multiple perspectives may be called on to take a stand, and I expect that many people will choose to stand in solidarity with gay, lesbian, bisexual, and transgender people."

If schism occurs in mainline denominations, Leslie feels it is unlikely that MCC parishioners will rush back to their old denominations in a great homecoming. "While MCC remains a church that is primarily a ministry to and by gay, lesbian, bisexual, and transgender people, there is far more to our denomination than identity politics."

However, reality has already begun to supercede hypothesis. Several ministers reported that Welcoming mainline denominations in their communities, in a surprising round of "turnabout," have begun to draw members from local MCC churches. In fact, Charleston's Metropolitan Community Church recently lost its pastor shortly before the Circular Church, a local United Church of Christ congregation, voted unanimously in favor of "Open and Affirming" designation after many months of education on gay and lesbian issues. If, in one of the most antigay states in the country, faith communities are able to open their doors to openly gay and lesbian Christians, the possibility remains that we will witness the realization of MCC founder Troy Perry's thirty-year-old dream—that ultimately, affirming attitudes toward homosexual orientation will eradicate the need for his denomination.

As increasing numbers of faith communities struggle with issues of inclusiveness, bridges will be needed to ensure that Christians of many sensibilities can adapt to unpredictable changes. Meg Riley (Chapter 4), a Unitarian Universalist minister, sees herself as such a bridge. Regarding sexual orientation issues within the Unitarian tradition, the most significant controversy—hardly one likely to cause schism—is the refusal of some clergy to sign legal marriage papers for heterosexual couples until same-sex couples can legally marry. Still, relative stability within the Unitarian Universalist tradition doesn't leave Meg unaffected by rifts in other denominations. "My calling is to hold things together, bridge gaps," she says. "Within my denomination, this is much more needed around race and class issues than sexual orientation. However, in interfaith coalitions, I am often the lesbian bridge that people walk across to feel okay about themselves and about their denominations. Sometimes, that means I am the recipient of the anguish they feel about the lack of faith they experience in their denominations."

Rev. Michael Hopkins (Chapter 3) foresees many fervent attempts to head off potential schism. "But two things are clear. The train of full inclusion has long ago left the station, and those who are not on it refuse to compromise their position in any way. Appeals to unity will, in the end, be quite ineffective."

A new dividing line, Michael says, is being drawn within Christianity. "Primarily, it has to do with the issue of biblical interpretation," he continues. "We have the beginning of a kind of new reformation. Clearly, it is happening in almost every denomination."

What does a "new reformation" mean for the next century? "That isn't clear," he says. "Will we simply have two branches of every denomination? Or will there be a literal re-formation of denominational splits? At this point, it's difficult to tell."

An Episcopal priest-in-exile feels that conservative groups within most faith communities have made it clear that homosexuality is a non-negotiable item. "Our current bishop seems determined to prevent schism during his presidency," says Harry Scott Coverston (Chapter 3). "Most of his statements are muffled in tone and restrained in substance. But it will take only one vote of the General Convention to approve creation of same-sex union rites to provoke the first cannon shots over Fort Sumter within the ECUSA." In fact, Harry is convinced that "conservatives are looking for a symbolic but clear signal that their time to depart has come. They will want an opportunity to leave, claiming the high ground of tradition and morality"—an emerging pattern that is evident in most denominations.

Ironically, a schism in the ECUSA might translate into an active place for Harry, whose Central Florida bishop is outspokenly antigay. "Frankly, if there is a schism, I believe—as a former lawyer—that many of the properties of the church will be tied up in litigation for years and will be ultimately sold to pay legal fees," he explains. "Should the situation change in this diocese where a faithful remnant is left after a schism, I would gladly devote myself to its survival and rebuilding."

Until that time, the door is closed on any official ministry for Harry within his diocese. Still, he continues his role as a spiritual leader. "A small group of refugees from the diocese, both straight and gay, meets in our home weekly for study, a common meal, Eucharist, and socializing," Harry says. "In many ways, this cell group/home church we call the Francis-Clare Community is a return to the earliest roots of the church in a postinstitutional age. The Internet is full of Web pages of small, catholic worshiping cell groups and home churches like the Francis-Clare Community. The Christian movement is clearly in a time of change. ECUSA's woes are only the more visible expressions of divisions and animosities affecting most mainline religious bodies today. In many ways, Christianity is undergoing a second reformation."

Jim Bilbrey, senior pastor at Universal Life Church in Columbus, Indiana, cautions faith communities struggling with gay and lesbian issues to realize there may be a narrow window of reconciliation during "Reformation 2000." From his perspective of the current state of affairs, he offers a chance for bridge building with a unique analogy. "In our twenty-five years of marriage, my wife and I have had few issues on which we differ this much," Jim says. "This is a big one. Cindy feels that because I am an ordained minister, I should know that homosexual relationships are immoral. She believes that when I officiate at a wedding for gay people, I am wrong, because gays should not be able to get married. She believes any gay sexual relationship to be a sin. She said she prays to God to show her if she is wrong in her beliefs, but she's heard nothing new from Him."

But in his continued studies of scriptures, Jim has learned that sex for all people, regardless of orientation and within the context of a devoted, monogamous relationship, can be a blessing from God. "And like my wife, I have prayed to God to show me if my beliefs are wrong. God says to me, 'It is not a sin.'"

What kind of bridge could establish reasonable peace in their marriage—a marriage Jim says that was once threatened by the depth of their disagreement? "Our biggest differences were in our religious views, and [in those views] we found the bridge," Jim continues. "We both love the Lord. Through Christ, we are united and affirmed in love. We have amicably agreed to disagree on the issue of gay and lesbian relationships. We do not enter into a gay-related conversation without first reaffirming our love in Christ. We are always honest and say what we think, but we don't speak from atop a soapbox. I am motivated to maintain a sturdy bridge of communication in my home because I am in love with my wife. I am not in love with The American Family Association or the Christian Coalition. It is hard for me not to think of groups such as these as The Enemy. But as the saying goes, 'It is hard to shake hands with a clenched fist.' Only God can help me maintain Christlike communication with them."

Ultimately, Jim believes, church families will change. God will make a "new creation," according to God's own timetable. However, for gay and lesbian Christians, the snail's pace of change might seem, at times, intolerable. "You who are gay Christians have my deepest admiration," he says. "You are under attack by the religious-political extremists because they think gays and lesbians can't be Christians. To them, you are perverts who should 'change.' You are also under attack by people in the gay community who think you have betrayed them. To them, you are Uncle Toms. I sometimes wonder how you maintain your faith under such persecution. Then, I understand that it is your faith in God that carries you through. The God who created you perfect, in His image, supplies you with sufficient grace for the journey. However people may argue with your understanding of scripture, they cannot argue with what you know is true in your heart. What the Lord has done in your heart is between you and your Creator. No amount of picking apart scripture can touch what the Lord has done there."

NOTES

Chapter 1: The Scheme of Things

1. Marcus J. Borg, *Meeting Jesus Again for the First Time: The Historical Jesus and the Heart of Contemporary Faith* (New York: HarperSanFrancisco, 1994), 125.
2. Interview with Professor Elizabeth Clark appears on the official Web site for the Public Broadcasting System (www.pbs.org) in association with the series *Frontline* ("From Jesus to Christ: Why Did Christianity Succeed?"), 1998.
3. Interview with Dr. Helmut Koester appears on the official PBS Web site.
4. Rodney Stark, "The Rise of Christianity: A Sociologist Reconsiders History," Public Broadcasting System (1998); from official PBS Web site.
5. The quotations of Duane Simolke that follow are from his *Reactions to Homophobia* (Baltimore: Overdrive Press, 1997), excerpted from his personal Web site.
6. Mike Silverman, "Gays and the Bible," in *Perceptual Fix* (On-line magazine), July 1998.
7. Peter J. Gomes, *The Good Book: Reading the Bible with Mind and Heart* (New York: William Morrow & Co., 1998), 148–57.
8. The quotations of John M. House that follow are from his *The Bible and Homosexuality* (Fort Lauderdale: Acropolis Publishing, 1990), excerpted from Body of Christ Church Web site (www.boc.org.).
9. Borg, *Meeting Jesus Again,* 59.
10. As reported by the News Odyssey Poll in *Business Wire* (September 17, 1998).
11. The quotations of Christopher Ott that follow are from, "God's Own ZIP Code," in *Salon* (On-line magazine), July 9, 1998.
12. The quotations of Jay Alan Sekulow that follow are from "Chief Counsel's Confidential Report on the Homosexual Agenda." Pamphlet issued via direct mail by the American Center for Law and Justice.
13. Donald E. Wildmon, "Principles Which Guide AFA's Opposition to the Gay Agenda." Report issued by the American Family Association, July 24, 1998.
14. *Homosexuality in America: Exposing the Myths* (Tupelo, MS.: American Family Association, 1996), 2–6.
15. "The Homosexual Movement: A Response by the Ramsey Colloquium," *First Things* 41 (March 1994): 15–21.

Chapter 2: Witnessing in Exile

1. Justin Chinn, "Our Reporter Survives the Ex-Gay Ministries," *The Progressive* 59, no.12 (December 1995): 32–35.
2. Daniel A. Helminiak, in a brochure written for Dignity/USA (1996) entitled "Catholicism, Homosexuality and Dignity."
3. Official newsletter of the Gay and Lesbian Alumni of the University of Notre Dame and Saint Mary's College (Spring 1998).
4. John M. Haas, "Catholic Church Invites Homosexuals to Choose Life," *Boston Globe* (February 25, 1998).
5. Tony and Peggy Campolo, "Is the Homosexual My Neighbor?" A transcript of a videotape of a talk delivered at North Park Chapel College on February 29, 1998.

Chapter 3: Prophets amid Tumult

1. Fully 83 percent of twenty-five partnered ministers interviewed indicated they would marry their partners if same-sex marriage were an option.
2. "Gay Christians Seek Church's Understanding," The Associated Press News Service, July 19, 1998.
3. Doug LeBlanc, ed., "Heat and Light at Burning Issues," *United Voice* (March 1998).
4. Guido Gagliano, "Gay Ordination Case Proceeds to Trial," *Christianity Today* 39,12 (October 2,1995): 107.
5. "The Episcopal Church and Homosexuality," Religious Tolerance Web site (www.religioustolerance.org),1996.
6. Notes from the Court for the Trial of a Bishop (May 15, 1996), found on Religious Tolerance Web site.
7. From a series of full-page ads in Delaware, Tennessee, Oregon, and Washington State newspapers purchased by conservative elements in the Episcopal Church USA (March 1996).
8. R. R. Reno, "Good Restaurants in Gomorrah," *First Things* (February 1998): 14–16.
9. John W. Kennedy, "Episcopal Bishops Divided Over Sexuality," *Christianity Today* 38,11 (October 3,1994): 70.
10. Notes from the convention of the Episcopal Diocese of Pennsylvania (1996) found on the Religious Tolerance Web site.
11. Diego Ribadeneira, "Episcopal Bishop Listens to All Sides," *Boston Globe* (February 21, 1998).
12. From official Lambeth Conference Resolution on Sexuality, issued August 1998.
13. Charles Henderson, "Homosexuality and the Bible," *The Mining Company*, September 15, 1997.
14. "Chicago Pastor Elected Moderator" (sidebar), *Christianity Today* 40, no. 12 (August 12, 1996): 56.

15. Patricia Rice, "Presbyterians Debate Ordination of Homosexuals," *St. Louis Post-Dispatch* (March 21, 1998).
16. Paul Nowell, "Presbyterians Hope to Squelch Debate on Sexuality Issue at National Meeting," Associated Press (June 12, 1998).
17. Jerry Van Marter, "Stotts Urges Covenant Network to Persevere," PCUSA News (June 15, 1998).
18. From the official Web site of "That All May Freely Serve"(www.tamfs.org).
19. "Lutheran Outreach with Lesbians and Gays," ELCA News Service, May 30, 1996.
20. "Vocations of Gay and Lesbian Lutherans," ELCA News Service, March 17, 1997.
21. Ibid.
22. H. George Anderson and Charles H. Maahs, "An Open Letter from the Bishops of the Evangelical Lutheran Church in America," *The Lutheran* (April 1996). Letter released March 22, 1996.
23. Martha Irvine, "Gay Clergy Challenge Church Policy," Associated Press (December 26, 1997).
24. Ibid.
25. Laura Clark, "Christianity and Homosexuality Co-Exist at Two Northland Churches," *Pitchweekly* (July 9–15, 1998).
26. "ELCA Bishops: Prayer and Encouragement for Gay Members," ELCA News Service, March 25, 1996.
27. On May 17,1999, Steve Sabin reported that the congregation council determined that the guilty verdict of being a "practicing homosexual" did not imply guilt of an offense of doctrine, morality, or continued neglect of duty. "These are the only three grounds recognized by our congregational constitution for removing a pastor," Steve explains. "Therefore, the council took no action." Meanwhile, Hougen told the congregation and others publicly that he intends to take no action against Lord of Life—at this time. "He told me that while the rules give him no discretion regarding me, he does have discretion regarding the congregation," Steve adds. "We are getting lots of new members."

Chapter 4: Visionaries in a New Land

1. From the official Unitarian Universalist Association (UUA) Web site (www.uua.org).
2. John Shelby Spong, *Why Christianity Must Change or Die: A Bishop Speaks to Believers in Exile* (New York: HarperSanFrancisco, 1998).
3. From official UUA Web site.
4. Max L. Stackhouse, "Same-Sex Unions? No: The Prophetic Stand of the Ecumenical Churches on Homosexuality," from official United Church of Christ (UCC) Web site (www.ucc.org). Dr. Stackhouse's paper was first given at a conference at Brown University and will appear in a vol-

ume to be published by Harvard University Press, *Religion and Same-Sex Marriage,* edited by S. Olyan and M. Nussbaum.

5. Andrew G. Lang, "Same-Sex Unions? Yes: The Order of Christian Covenant in Marriage, Celibacy and Same-Sex Unions," from official UCC Web site.

6. John M. Glionna, "A Path Less Traveled," *Los Angeles Times* (March 16, 1998).

Chapter 5: Reformation 2000

1. "Preachers of Hate" (a commentary), *The Progressive* 62,12 (December 1998): 8.

2. From an Internet clearinghouse of the positions of all faith communities regarding homosexual issues. The clearinghouse is located at www.religioustolerance.com.

3. Guy Trebay, "Beyond the Fence: Conjuring the Lives of Martyr Matthew Shepard," *Village Voice* (October 28–November 3, 1998).

4. From the official Affirmation: United Methodists for Gay, Lesbian, Bisexual, and Transgendered Concerns Web site (www.umaffirm.org/cornews/creech.html).

5. Ann Rodgers-Melnick, "Schism Over Homosexuals Feared," *Toledo Blade* (April 30, 1998).

6. American Family Radio News Service, March 24, 1999.

7. As reported by the Knight Ridder News Service, December 4, 1998.

8. Farewell Address printed in *Anglican Voice* (March 1998).

9. Issued by James H. Thrall, reporting for the Episcopal News Service.

10. From Davenport's letter posted on the official University Baptist Church Web site (www.ubcaustin.org/ubc.htm).

11. John Shelby Spong, *Why Christianity Must Change or Die: A Bishop Speaks to Believers in Exile* (New York: Harper San Francisco,1998).